To Joel & Betty

I Won't Survive …
I'll Thrive!

D1111752

I am so happy
To have you both
as new Friends.

Live your Legacy!

Love you,

Ann

Proverbs 14:3

I Won't Survive ...
I'll Thrive!

✦

How I Overcame Domestic Violence, Cancer, and Much More

Aurea McGarry

iUniverse, Inc.
New York Lincoln Shanghai

I Won't Survive ... I'll Thrive!
How I Overcame Domestic Violence, Cancer, and Much More

iUniverse books may be ordered through booksellers or by contacting:

iUniverse
2021 Pine Lake Road, Suite 100
Lincoln, NE 68512
www.iuniverse.com
1-800-Authors (1-800-288-4677)

Because of the dynamic nature of the Internet, any Web addresses or links contained in this book may have changed since publication and may no longer be valid.

ISBN: 978-0-595-45369-6 (pbk)
ISBN: 978-0-595-69709-0 (cloth)
ISBN: 978-0-595-89680-6 (ebk)

Printed in the United States of America

The views expressed in this work are solely those of the author and do not necessarily reflect the views of the publisher, and the publisher hereby disclaims any responsibility for them.

CREDITS

1. "What happens to a dream ..." quote from the 1951 poem "Harlem," by Langston Hughes, as used in the 1959 play *A Raisin in the Sun,* by Lorraine Hansberry.

2. Scripture: all scripture taken from the New King James version ... © 1979, 1980, 1982, by Thomas Nelson, Inc., used by permission. All rights reserved.

3. Poem: One Flaw in Women, Author Unknown

This book is a work of non-fiction. However, the names and other identifying information of certain individuals have been changed to protect their privacy. The changes do not impact the accuracy of the events described. In writing this book, I have tried to share some of my life experiences that I hope others will benefit from. It is in no way intended to emotionally hurt or defame the character of any persons, either living or dead.

An amazing real life story sure to inspire you! Aurea is not defined by her suffering, but by her faith and joy of living. She'll teach you how you can make life-changing choices even when your situation appears hopeless. Thriving is a 100 percent proposition in her life. It can be in yours, too.

Marla Eurick
Life coach for entrepreneurs.

A fascinating story of what faith can do when continuous tragic matters strike every family member. McGarry in her exceptional book, "I Won't Survive … I'll Thrive!" displays her tenaciousness and passion for life that can facilitate her readers not only to overcome their own dilemmas and disasters, but turning it into an awe-inspiring gain.

Tatiana Victoria Pahlen Poet/Writer, New York City

This book is presented to:

_____

From:

_____

Date:

_____

In loving memory of my mother

Barbara Faltraco
1934–1994

My mother was my biggest cheerleader, my best friend, and a wonderful grandmother to my daughter. She gave me an amazing childhood and guided me through my journeys in life that helped mold me into the wife, mother and person that I am today. I miss her so much.

To my husband, Brian McGarry.

Brian, you are my Prince Charming, my knight in shining armor, my soul mate, the wind beneath my wings, and my true north. I thank you for saving my life in so many ways. I am glad to have been given a chance to grow old with you and watch you become a "daddy" to our granddaughter. Without your daily help, this book would not have been possible. I love you!

Contents

List of Illustrations

Acknowledgments

1. My stepfather, Eric … you were my mother's Prince Charming and made her last years happy ones. I thank you for that and so much more.

2. My brother, Doric … you were my hero and father figure growing up, and I always wanted to make you proud of me. I hope I have.

3. My sister, Anthia … you have taught me many lessons in life. Although we have grown apart, you are still my sister, and I love you.

4. My grandmother, Margaret … you taught me about heaven and God's love, and to love poetry and books. Well, Grams, I finally wrote my book.

5. My daughter, Angelica … you are beautiful and sing like an angel. We have been through so much together. You have taught me about style and fashion, and what it means to be a mother. I would lay down my life for you.

6. My newest family member, my sweet grandchild, Alyssa … may you learn from my heartaches and pitfalls so your life can be so much greater.

7. My mother-in-law, Norma Jean McGarry … for never missing any of my chemo treatments and for making sure I had the best doctors possible. You are one of God's angels.

8. The entire McGarry family … you all have been so good to Angelica and I from the day we met. You help Brian and I pursue our dreams, and I am so glad we are family.

9. My business mentor, Mary Jones … you helped me to achieve success beyond my wildest dreams. You are my teacher, nurse, second mom, and friend. Thanks for always believing in me.

10. My friend, Lisa Skinner … for twenty-six years, we have been there for each other. You will always be my best friend, because you know too much.

11. My editor and friend, Virginia Davis ... you kept my nose to the grindstone and encouraged me to keep writing this book—even when life kept happening for us both.

And last, but certainly not least, Jesus Christ, to whom I gave my heart and soul at the age of twenty-two. You gave me the gift of life more than once, and the gift of salvation. My life of service is my gift back to you. I believe you when you say in Jeremiah 29:11, "You know the plans you have for us, to bless and prosper and not harm us."

Prologue

The cold January wind whipped about my friend Patty's face and mine as we rushed up Forty-second Street. We pulled our scarves closer around our mouths and did not try to talk above the whistling wind. Just before we left school today, I was telling Patty that today was my father's birthday, and I didn't know if he would be spending it with us or in Boston. I had a gift for him but had not mailed it, hoping that he would be with us on his birthday. I knew my siblings had gifts for him, too.

As we rounded the corner, I saw a few twinkling Christmas lights still blinking from some of the trees on the street and from a few windows. I suppose people had left them up, as if refusing to succumb to winter's gray and bleakness. Only a month earlier, the great tree had sparkled in Rockefeller Center, and the windows at Saks and Tiffany's had been decorated as Christmas cards that took your breath away. Then, on New Year's Eve in Times Square, the world again had waited with Dick Clark for the giant ball to drop and usher in 1977. Those were happy memories for a fifteen-year-old girl to recall as we rushed toward home in anticipation of a warm fire and hot cocoa.

Patty and I giggled as we tried to see who could get through my front door first. Mother was in the kitchen.

"I'm freezing," I shouted to her, as I dropped my coat, scarf, gloves and books in the foyer. Patty did the same.

As I entered the kitchen, I stopped. The look on my mother's face told me that something terrible was wrong.

"What's wrong?" I asked. "Mom, what has happened?"

"Sit down, Aurea. I have something to tell you," she said.

I sat in a kitchen chair and felt Patty's hands on my shoulders.

"Honey," Mom began. "I should wait until your brother and sister get home and tell you all. But you will just be anxious, so … Honey, today your father was killed in an automobile accident in Boston."

I didn't think I had heard her correctly. *Killed?* But it is his birthday!

I was thinking about making a card for him to go with the gift. Surely he wasn't gone. Maybe there was a mistake. My brother and sister came home, and each was shocked with the news, as I had been. After a few minutes of silence and

1

a few questions, we kids all went up to our own rooms to absorb the news. After trying to assure herself that I was coping, Patty finally went home.

I heard Mother talking endlessly on the telephone. Was she making some funeral arrangements? What was she saying?

I snuck out of my room and held my ear to the door of her room.

"I told the kids he died in an automobile accident," I could hear her say.

Now I knew there was more to the story. Some friends had brought in food, so Mother called us down to dinner. But none of us felt much like eating.

"Mother, is there something you aren't telling us?" I asked.

She looked into my eyes, and she knew that I suspected that she wasn't telling everything.

"I'm sorry I didn't tell you children the truth, but the way he died is so horrible," she said. "I wanted to spare you. But you all can read, and it will be in all the papers, so you might as well hear it from me. Your father was killed—murdered. Shot twice in the back of his head and thrown out of a car. He was found lying dead on the side of the road by two hitchhikers."

The world was spinning. I thought I heard my sister scream, but I wasn't sure. *Murdered?* That was something you read about in the newspapers, or saw on television, or maybe in the movies. It didn't happen in real life—not to the people you knew and loved.

Murdered? I felt sick at my stomach. This wasn't happening—it wasn't real. How could a man, an important man, be killed on his birthday! He was fifty-seven years old today. He would walk through that door and we would sing "Happy Birthday." Oh, Daddy … oh, poor Daddy!

I felt a shudder pass over my body and the little hairs on my neck stand up. It was as if I was having a premonition. Yes, I knew that from this day forward, our lives would never be the same. January 28, 1977, was the end of our Camelot and the day our world changed forever.

PART I

1

A New Life

The day I was born—October 7, 1961—was a crisp, beautiful autumn day in Manhattan. The sun was golden and casting a glow about everything. The golden hue spilled through the hospital windows, and that is, perhaps, another reason why my father, George E. George, decided to name his baby girl Aurea.

The real reason was that "Aurea" means "beautiful" in Greek, and my middle name—Colleen—means "girl" in Irish, my mother's roots.

"She has hair like spun gold!" my mother said as she smiled.

I was the third baby born to George and Barbara. Even though I didn't know it yet, I was born with a silver spoon in my mouth.

My father had come to America from Greece. He and his family had come to Ellis Island when he was just a boy, and they settled in Shelby, Ohio, where others of their family had migrated. George had graduated from Harvard University in 1943 as one of the top ten in his class. He received his Bachelor of Law degree form George Washington University in 1948.

My father was a hard worker and made a lot of money in the stock market and by opening and running his own shipping companies. He associated with the likes of Dwight D. Eisenhower, Margaret Truman, and Richard Nixon's private secretary, Rose Mary Woods. As a very successful lawyer and savvy businessman, he made millions of dollars. He wanted his family to have the best of everything, and we did.

My mother, Barbara, was a gorgeous blonde who modeled for *Cosmopolitan* magazine in the 1950s and was a Chef Boyardee and Prell Shampoo commercial spokesmodel as well. She also earned her living as a legal secretary with extremely fast typing skills. She had met George at a party in Washington, D.C. He was a wealthy business tycoon and she was a successful model. She had made money of her own but would soon give it all up to be a stay-at-home mom. They had a whirlwind romance and Daddy swept her off her feet, showering her with everything money could buy. The proposal of marriage with a glamorous life in a big city was next. Just the thought of moving to New York City was my mother's dream come true.

They bought a five-story townhouse on the east side of Eighty-sixth Street near Carl Schultz Park. They loved their new place for seven years, then moved to an apartment on Park Avenue when I was around two years old. Although they were leaving a large luxurious town home, Mother got tired of chasing us kids up and down five flights of stairs all day.

So, with parents that were like shining icons to me, my world would be golden and filled with sunshine. As a newborn, I took it all in stride and smiled like a cherub; after all, it was my birthright, and life was grand.

So I grew with love and self-confidence.

2

Cupsey to the Rescue

I was the baby of the family, and my mother doted over me, as mothers tend to do over their youngest. Doric was their firstborn and a leader from the very beginning, and my sister Anthia was the mischievous middle child.

Two can be a difficult age, and just the age when children can start showing some of their independence. Anthia probably couldn't understand all this fuss over her new baby sister. Her mother had always bounced Anthia on her lap, but now there was a new little girl on Mommy's lap.

One day, when I was two and my sister was four-and-a-half, I was in the play area, chasing a ray of sunshine across the floor. I would try to catch the dust particles in my hand as they drifted toward the window to be swallowed by the ray of sun going back to heaven. I laughed while doing this, and the sound of my laughter drew Anthia into my room. Doric's baseball bat was leaning against the wall in the corner of the play area. She picked up the bat, held it over her head and came running toward me. Suddenly out of nowhere came Cupsey, my mother's protective German shepherd. The dog grabbed Anthia by the ear and pulled her to floor just before the bat hit my head. Poor Anthia—she screamed and screamed. Mother rushed her to the hospital for several stitches in her ear.

This event was the beginning of my passion for dogs, experiencing first-hand their protective nature. And this would not be the last time our family dog would try to protect me. It was only about a year later, when my sister and I were having lunch at our kitchen table, that our heroic dog would again sense danger.

While Mother turned her back on us for a moment to answer the telephone, Anthia poured a whole bottle of baby aspirin into my glass of milk. Cupsey was the only one who saw what she had done and, with her keen senses, realized something was wrong with that. She ran to the table and pushed over the glass of milk, as my mom frantically turned around from the sound of the crashing glass, she saw the undissolved aspirins in the milk scattered all over the table. From that day on, Mother never turned her back on us again, knowing that it only takes a second for children to get hurt.

These and many other family anecdotes where told over and over again at our dinner table meals and embedded in my mind the wonderful place that animals have in our lives. We had so many happy times as a family, and I have many old home movies that recorded the fun. Mother loved all animals, and I inherited that love of animals from her.

Once, in Carl Schultz Park, some baby squirrels had fallen out of a tree. There were some mean boys throwing rocks at them for fun. Most of the squirrels escaped, but my mother picked up one extremely small one and told the boys to be on their way. She brought the squirrel home, and we named it Spanky. He was so cute. Mother would bathe Spanky in the kitchen sink with a toothbrush. After the bath, Spanky would run all over the apartment and then sit on Daddy's head to unwind from all the excitement. If there had been a show of America's funniest videos back then, I know Spanky's video would have won.

After living in the five-story townhouse, we moved to Park Avenue for two years, then we moved to my favorite apartment building on Eighty-sixth Street, where we would spend the next eleven years. There was a great pool and spa in the basement there, and we were always running into celebrities. Those were some of the happiest years of my life.

My mother, Barbara Gayle Runion, modeling for Chef Boyardee commercials in the 1950s.

My father, George E. George.

My brother, Doric, with my sister Anthia in the middle—and me on the end—when we lived on Park Avenue.

3

Skating with the Stars

Lake Placid is a beautiful place to spend the summer. It is a mecca for ice skaters, and it was where my brother Doric, Mother, and I spent our summers. Our sister enjoyed boarding camp in New Jersey.

I began skating at the age of three and was the youngest member of the New York City skating club at the time. We stayed in resorts in Lake Placid, skating eight hours a day. From skating, I learned early the importance of self-discipline and hard work. I loved the bright costumes and had one with yellow and gold feathers. My long hair almost reached my skates; when I would twirl my hair would spread out in a huge fan. I didn't feel elegant and golden, but my parents said I was.

But I just liked being a tomboy.

The big Labor Day Ice Show was what we practiced for all summer. All the parents came to see it. I skated in the show along with Dorothy Hamill, Dick Button, Janet Lynn and many others who would star in the Olympics in later years.

Back in the city, I would skate every day. I loved it. I would watch the world blur past me as I sped across the ice, feeling like the little ballerina skater that twirls when you open a child's jewelry box. As I gradually became an accomplished figure skater, I just knew that one day I would be a star.

I loved to skate to music—even more than doing the figures. The music made me want to skate fast and feel as if I was flowing across the ice. I loved performing for an audience. It was hard work skating at such a young age, and everyone was older than me, so I had to be very good and fast to fit in. I was always the youngest and smallest at all the ice shows, but didn't want to be the smallest skater—I wanted to be the greatest.

My father took us to Lake Placid in the summer. Doric and I both skated and took private lessons in figure skating and ice dancing. We knew we would not see our father again until the Labor Day show, and we worked hard to be able to show off for him. Father had important work in the city, and he made a wonderful living for us. But sometimes we missed his attention.

I was very close to my mother. She always told me I could do anything, and I still remember the smell of her "Joy" perfume. Dad always gave her a new bottle of "Joy" for Christmas, and she wore it as sparingly as gold dust.

I was so close to my mother that around age five, I began having nightmares about losing her in a dark movie theater. In the dream, I would run through the dark theater halls looking for her, and then I would see her far off, at the end of a dark hallway. I'd try to call out to her, but no words would come out of my mouth. I would wake up from those dreams very upset. So when I was five, Mother gave me a 14K gold charm bracelet: the charms were an ice skate, a mouse, an angel with my birthstone, and a very special little worry bird. Mother told me the little worry bird would wrinkle up its forehead and do all my worrying for me, so I wouldn't have to. She said I was smart and beautiful; she became my biggest cheerleader and best friend. Even as an adult, I still wear this charm bracelet on special occasions.

Me at age seven, posing for the big Labor Day photo shoot in my yellow
bird costume.

4

Unlucky Thirteen

When I was six, I was enrolled in a very elite, private, predominately Jewish school near our home. I thought I would love school, because I learned quickly and loved meeting new friends, but the first grade teacher was mean to me because I wasn't Jewish, like all the other kids in my class that year. She made me feel unwelcome, and I was afraid to go to school a lot that year. Once the second grade rolled around, though, that teacher was nice to me, and I liked her a lot; she made learning much more fun.

At the time, I had no idea the school cost $35,000 a year for each of us children to attend. We lived in a plush New York apartment on the east side and rode around in limousines. I remember reading the book *Eloise* by Kay Thomson. I guess most little girls envied the book's character, being able to live in the plaza and having a diplomat for a father, but I didn't. My own life was more fascinating than hers.

In 1968, my mother divorced my father. I was only seven years old, and it was devastating to me. I didn't understand what divorce really meant or why it was happening, but I was the only child in the second grade to have divorced parents, and the other kids ridiculed me for it. In the 1960s, divorce wasn't as common as today, and children my age didn't really know what it was. All I knew was that adults said it was something bad, and the kids made me feel as if *I* had done something wrong. I was lucky that my second-grade teacher was much nicer and more understanding than the one I'd had a year earlier.

My parents' marriage had lasted for thirteen years. I guess thirteen was their unlucky number.

Dad was gone a lot because of his business, and he did not stay with us for most of our summers in Lake Placid. Dad had grown up in an unaffectionate family that found it difficult to show love. Mother liked hugs, kisses, and sweet words, but they simply were not my father's way. He showered her with gifts and everything money could buy, but he was gone on business for weeks at the time—it was the price he paid to make millions.

I don't know why he had affairs with other women. I am certain they were not as beautiful as my mother, with her flowing blond hair and her five foot seven model body. And I know he did not love them. I suspect they were only an antidote to his loneliness, but I was far too young to understand those things then.

After years of this, my mother grew weary and hired detectives to follow my father and obtain proof of his affairs. Information like that was necessary in the 1960s to get a divorce with alimony. She went to Mexico and got a quick divorce, wanting to spare her children the pain of a drawn-out court battle. She was awarded a handsome alimony and child support settlement. I asked my mother if I should still call him "Daddy," and she said, "Of course."

Daddy came on the weekends and took us swimming, to the toy store, and out to dinner. We always had fun when he came to see us. Not seeing my father much meant I needed a male role model, and my brother quickly filled the role.

Doric was tall, dark, and handsome and excelled in everything he did. He was a songwriter, musician, singer, dancer, actor, and scholar, and he was funny. He became the life of every party and could do stand-up comedy routines for hours. By the time Doric was sixteen, he was in a band, and all the girls were crazy about him. But he still found time to help me with my homework and make me feel important. In my eyes, he was perfect. All my life, I wanted to make him proud of me; his smile and praise became what I lived for. My girlfriends all loved him, too, so our home was a very popular place for girls to hang out.

After my parents' divorce, some of the other kids at school were so cruel to me that Mother enrolled me into a new school: Marymount, a private, all-girls Catholic school near our apartment, on Fifth Avenue overlooking Central Park. The kids there didn't know anything about my parents' divorce at first, so it was easier to come in and make friends quickly before they found out.

I did very well in that school for six years. Mom was Catholic but feared the church because the nuns had been mean to her growing up in the 1940s. Dad and we kids were Protestant, but Marymount was one of the best private schools in the city.

I was very happy in that school and made friends with whom I still stay in contact.

My brother, Doric.

5

Grams

After the divorce, I often saw my mother upset and crying. At the time, I couldn't understand why. All I knew is that I wanted her to smile and be happy, and I wanted to take care of her. So we grew even closer as I spent lots of time doing fun things with her.

My grandmother was Margaret Runion. She was my mother's mother, and she came to live with us after the divorce to help my mother and provide moral support.

She was a great lady, and I could talk to her about anything, especially God. Grandmother (we called her Grams) was so smart and loved to read novels. She was a fast reader and could get through an entire book in just one day. Her favorite books were the Bible and mysteries—Agatha Christie was one of her favorite authors. I remember constantly seeing those books all over the house.

Grams also loved poetry and would read it for hours, and even write her own poems and plays, usually as well as any screenplay that received rave reviews in her local paper. I always wished I had inherited her love for reading. I was always so active; I loved sports and could never sit still, so Grams helped with my school book reports, which I hated writing. I'm sure she would be pleased and surprised to know I'm writing a book and enjoying reading much more now as an adult.

My grandmother was a wonderful Christian woman, and it was through her that I first learned what it meant to have faith in God and to love Jesus. I remembered her teachings and all the Bible stories she told me. Grandmother was the oldest of four girls and had been a singer in her younger years. She and her three sisters composed a quartet around the same time the Andrews Sisters were famous. When I would see the Andrews Sisters in a film or on television, I would always think of my grandmother. She lived with us for six years before she moved back to Chevy Chase, Maryland—her hometown—to be with her sister. Chevy Chase was the town in which my mother had been raised, and I visited her often on a five-hour bus ride from the city.

This is my grandmother's poem that she wrote in 1928:

Promises

I watched the dawn flame in the sky
and from my heart went up a cry
of joy supreme.
I listened for the birds' first call,
Breezes stirred and dew began to fall …
All nature sang—"God (love) is all."

I watched the sunset's crimson glow,
I watched till I began to know
A soothing presence and a quiet peace;
The sunset merged to a somber gray and thus had passed—another
    day.

I watched a full moon climb the sky
and saw the shadows flitting by,
I knew the stars' beckoning lights
Promised hope to climb the heights—of life.

Awake with dawn—live life anew,
God is love … respond … be true,
Revive the good within you sleeping lay—
Revive it at the break of day.
Watch the sunset crimson glow
From the heart begins to flow gratitude—
Because you find the means to quiet a troubled mind.

Gaze from your window every night,
look to the heavens beckoning lights.
There lies your strength to fight the fight
and win.

6

Precious Memories

I loved Mother so much; she was my best friend growing up.

As a young child, I would always ask her to stop smoking. I hated the smell of cigarette smoke. It was fashionable for women to smoke back then because everyone smoked in the movies and on television. Cigarette ads were on television and in all the magazines. Mother said she wished she had never started the nasty habit and wished she had the willpower to stop. She always told us how bad they were health-wise, but never forbade us to smoke; she knew that kids want to do what they're told not to. But none of us ever picked up the habit—somehow, even then, we knew they were very harmful. And anyway, they smelled so bad.

My mother and I had such fun together. Our favorite television show was *I Love Lucy*. We would cuddle and watch every episode, with a box of TV Munch chocolate candy. We would laugh until our sides almost split as the television actors and Lucy would clown around and act silly, a lot like my mom did.

Mother had her hair done at the Palace Hair Salon in New York City. One day when Mother and I were there, we met Lucille Ball. Lucy was under the dryer and she smiled and talked to us like she had known us for years. She was so sweet and kind—even while getting her hair done.

Meeting Lucy was a huge thrill for me, even though we were always running into celebrities in Manhattan. But seeing my favorite actress in person and sharing that moment with my mother was priceless.

Mom and I watched a lot of ice skating on television, too. We would go skating at Rockefeller Plaza, and we would stand on the street and watch the first of many Trump Towers being built. Shopping on Fifth Avenue was our favorite pastime.

Mother also loved teddy bears, and she and I collected them together. It was always so much fun when we were shopping and spotted a new bear. FAO Swartz was my favorite store as a child, as is the case with most children growing up in New York. Steiff and Gund bears were among our favorites. We would take the new teddy bear home with us and have fun naming it and finding a place to display it. Mom was the best at naming stuffed animals; I don't know where she came up with so many names. There was Pickles and Peepers and Agapo and Softie and Cuddles and Doctor Bear … she never ran out of names. We both continued to collect them throughout our entire adult years.

Late at night, we would watch old Gene Kelly movies, and if I was home from school sick, or on vacation, we would sit up and watch *The Tonight Show Starring Johnny Carson*. I thought it was cool staying up later than anyone, watching Johnny with my mom.

Another one of my favorite memories was watching Robert Redford swimming laps in the pool in the basement of our high-rise apartment building on Eighty-sixth street. I had a huge childhood crush on him at the time, and when he smiled and said "Hi" to me as he wrapped his wet body in a towel and passed me by to go up the stairs, my twelve-year-old heart almost burst. I walked around on a cloud for weeks.

My mother, in her late fifties—still glamorous—in a catalogue photograph.

7

Gone to the Dogs

I had learned to study hard, work hard, and play hard. I was filled with energy and always wanted to be doing something. Perhaps the work ethic and the need to be a young entrepreneur came from my father's genes. I was always thinking of ways to be working toward a goal, although we were already wealthy and I wanted for nothing.

One of my first jobs was at the ripe old age of eleven. We were still living in the luxury apartment on Eighty-sixth Street, and it seemed that almost everyone had a dog. I told the doorman at our building that I wanted to walk dogs. He got the word out for me, and in no time I had seven dogs to walk every day—once in the morning, before school, and then again after school. They were a mixture of breeds, from a gentle, sixty-pound Malamute to a tiny, smart Dachshund. I got up at 5:00 every morning and walked them in rain, sleet, snow, or summer sunshine. I managed to negotiate my pay to $1 a day per dog for the twice-walk routine. I loved to walk the dogs, because I loved to walk, I loved dogs, and I loved to work hard and make my own cash. The dogs liked me, too. I had a special bond with each one of them; I guess I was a very young *Dog Whisperer*.

We had some famous people living in our building, and one of my favorite clients was Dr. Joyce Brothers. I walked her sweet little cocker spaniel, Joey. Doctor Brothers was nice to me; she always gave me nice tips and invited me in to watch the taping of some of her TV shows, which were filmed in her apartment two floors above ours … It was all very exciting.

Dogs can be tricky, sometimes tangling up with each other in their leashes. But I usually walked them one at a time, which was much easier. Believe it or not, there *are* a few trees in Manhattan, and that's where the dogs pooped. And of course, the fire hydrants were always their favorite urinals. Thankfully for me, these were the days before pooper scooper laws.

There was so much noise and activity on the streets that my dogs seldom noticed cats or other dogs across the avenue. The dogs were lots of fun, and before long I was earning more than $50 a week. I was also learning how to manage money and how to save as well as spend. I was probably the only eleven-year-old in my posh school actually earning money as an entrepreneur.

8

Good-bye to Camelot

Much of an eight-year period of my life—age three to eleven—was spent figure skating, training, performing, ice dancing, and hoping to someday be good enough for the Olympics—or at least the Ice Capades.

But during the summer I was eleven, my father decided to reform a new shipping company, and he told us we would need to make some cuts in our expenses. We still lived luxuriously, but my three-month summers in Lake Placid came to an end.

"Don't worry," Mother told us at the time, "This is just for now. Soon things will be back to normal."

My whole self-esteem in school revolved around me being the best skater in school, and every year our school's Christmas party was a skating party at Rockefeller Center's skating rink. At the party, I was always the center of attention; all the kids, teachers, and parents watched me do spins and jumps. I wasn't the prettiest or smartest kid in school, and I already felt ostracized because of my parents' divorce, but once a year, I was a star—the class princess. It was a great comfort to me, and I would look forward to it all year long.

I was in New York for the first summer when I was twelve, and I started taking gymnastic classes at the YWCA. It was something I could pay for with my dog-walking money. The gymnastic classes kept me motivated and working toward another goal. My legs were strong from skating, so I learned fast. The balance beam was my favorite, because I had acquired great balance from all my ballet lessons.

After I had two years of gymnastics under my belt and was about to make the gymnastic team at age fourteen, my brother needed to move our couch. Thinking I was stronger than I actually was, I lifted one end of the couch and promptly hurt my back. I was in such pain that they took me to the hospital, where it was determined that I had slipped a disk and needed to be put into traction. All the apparatuses attached to my hospital bed made it look like a *Star Wars* spaceship.

My brother Doric helped out by making a skit with the bed being a fighter plane in battle, and it worked; I was soon laughing. Then they said the most awful words a teenager can hear: "bed pan." I started to cry, and I wanted to go home.

Mom talked the doctor into giving me a back brace that I could wear at home, but I would have to wear it for six weeks. And I was told I should never do backbends again, so my gymnastics career was already over. Another dream unfulfilled.

But I didn't give up. I would stay active and keep on moving and setting new goals. I loved to sing and dance, so I signed up for jazz and tap dancing classes on Broadway, at the famous Luigi's and Phil Black Studios, where many famous dancers had trained. I knew I had to stay motivated and have goals to strive for; it kept me strong. Living in Manhattan, I had the world at my fingertips, and I knew I would just keep redirecting my artistic goals until I was on the path to stardom and success—hopefully movies. It was always my nature to keep looking on the bright side and realizing that there would always be a tomorrow.

But one tomorrow that came brought unbelievable news: that my father was violently murdered, gangster-style they told us. Although they never found out exactly who did it, the mafia was implied. After a long investigation, the case was put on a back shelf, and to this day, my father's murder has never been solved. To make matters worse, due to the extenuating circumstances surrounding the murder, we were unable to collect any life insurance or assets, and we were left penniless.

Father's death was such a shock; it still didn't seem real. My brother shut himself in his room, and we didn't see much of him for those first few weeks after it happened. Doric is four years older than I, and my sister is two and a half years older. I remember kids at school bringing in the newspaper account of Father's death. Although my mother had not held a job for fifteen years when my father died, she was still able to return to work quickly, becoming a receptionist at a law firm. Although she had great typing skills and was very personable, there was no way she could make enough money to keep us in our apartment and pay for our expensive private schools. We would have to leave Manhattan.

The realization of that made me ill. Manhattan was all I had known. My mother rented a very small apartment in Queens. She apologized to us for having to move away and told us it was all she could afford but assured us that she would try to save some money so we could one day move back to Manhattan. She hated to leave as much as I did.

As spring arrived in 1977, with the frozen city beginning to thaw and the leaves on the trees in Central Park beginning to turn green, we loaded up all our possessions and the family dog, Admiral—our faithful, golden-brown, blue-eyed Siberian husky—and Happy, my favorite blue parakeet, into a yellow cab. With tears in our eyes, we waved good-bye to our doorman—and to our life as we had known it.

Ex-magnate's murder
shrouded in mystery

By GEORGE SOUZA

FRI FEB 4 - 1977   *Staff Writer*

Detectives are trying to unravel the mystery behind the gangland-style murder of a prominent Washington attorney and former multi-millionaire New York stockbroker whose body was found in the Blue Hills Reservation, Quincy, last Friday night, less than three hours after he arrived in Boston.

1968 Photo

The body of George Ezekial George 57, an alumnus of Harvard and George Washington University, with two bullets lodged in the back of the head, was found at 6:45 p.m. on the well-traveled **George** Wampatuck Road by two hitchhikers. He was last seen when he disembarked from a New York plane at Logan Airport at 4 p.m.

The body lay without identification until Monday, when his divorced wife, Barbara, viewed the body after MDC police detectives contacted her at her plush New York apartment.

Police theorize George may have been shot somewhere else and his body pushed onto the roadway from a car.

They immediately ruled out robbery as the motive as $200 was found on the body. They speculated he was an affluent man because he was dressed in a cashmere topcoat, a three piece corduroy suit and a muffler-scarf-glove set which one police official said "nobody can afford to wear anymore."

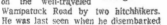

The body bore a few marks other than the bullet wounds, one of which pierced his brain and caused death, according to an autopsy.

The murder is under investigation by the MDC police. For the past week two MDC detectives, Sgt. Thomas Kehoe and Richard Horrigan, have been in New York attempting to find leads and a motive for the slaying.

"We first have to unravel his complex business deals. We brought back from New York carton after carton of his papers which indicate he was about to launch a new business. Each page we turn adds up to more millions of dollars," Horrigan said on his return to Boston last night.

DELVING INTO George's background, police found he graduated from Harvard in 1943, where he received his law degree, and from George Washington University in 1948.

He founded and owned Dewey, Johnson & George Inc., a New York brokerage firm, and became a millionaire several times over. But in 1973 he suffered financial setbacks and lost his fortune. He had divorced his wife a few years earlier. He leaves three children.

According to police, his business acumen was such that he was engaged by a number of prominent East Coast financial firms who found themselves in difficulties and quickly placed them back in the profit margin.

"All his business associates that we talked to in New York fully believed that he would be a millionaire again and in short time," Horrigan said.

They found that George was attempting to launch a new venture in shipping and the import-export business.

"According to his papers and talks with business people, George had sufficient backers to launch his new business. But we feel he had come to Boston to raise even more money," Horrigan said.

Newspaper article from Boston Newspaper

9

Sleepless in Queens

Once we had settled into our new apartment in Queens, it was only a few short weeks until my sister moved out. My brother soon followed. They had found a way to get back to Manhattan, because they were old enough to leave home. But I was determined to find a way for my mother and I to return too.

Mom had the job as a receptionist for a law firm in the city, and I helped out by making some money babysitting and dog walking in the same building where I had lived. I wasn't ready to let go of my former life altogether, so every day after school I went to walk or sit with the dogs while their owners were out of town. I tried to stay in the building as long as possible every night, and then take the subway back to Queens late in the evening. Sometimes if I had to work babysitting until 11:00 PM, I would go in the back area of the building's plush lobby—which was set up like a living room with couches, tables, and a glass sliding door leading out to the garden area—and sleep overnight. The doormen watched over me, sympathetic of how my life had abruptly changed. They didn't mind at all that I tried so desperately to hold on tight to a little piece of my past.

But sleeping at my old building wasn't just about holding onto the past. In our new Queens apartment, I was often visited by tiny, unwelcome roommates.

It was my first week in our new apartment, and one night I got up to get a drink of water. When I returned to my bedroom, I switched on the light. To my horror, I saw dozens of German cockroaches scurrying over my bed and blanket. I didn't scream; I wanted to remain calm for my mother, because I knew she was going through more than enough already. So calmly, I left my room that night and slept in a chair in the living room with a lamp turned on.

The next morning, Mom asked, "Aurea, why aren't you in your bed?"

"We need bug spray, Mom. We have roaches."

We bought the bug spray, but it didn't help. Unfortunately, we learned, if all your neighbors don't exterminate right along with you, the pests keep coming back. So I would sleep in the lobby of my old building or at a friend's house whenever possible. Otherwise, my nights at home were spent sleeping with a light on.

But I never stayed away from home for too long, because I didn't want my mom to worry about me—or to be alone.

Mom and I found an apartment back in the city through my best friend, Patty, who was from an Irish Catholic family with seven children. They lived in a high-rise apartment building only six blocks from where we had lived. Through the church, Mom and I were able to get on the list to buy one of the co-ops. Together, we did.

It was in that building that I met my first love. I met him while I was walking our husky just down the street from our building. I was still only fifteen, but he was an older man—nineteen—with blond hair and blue eyes. My own personal Robert Redford.

He was a handy man in our building, and he started dating a Spanish girl who lived in the building the same week he started dating me. I was his girl with big dreams, places to go, people to meet, and auditions to attend. I wanted to travel and do something important and big with my life. He, on the other hand, was not that ambitious, but he was great listener and a great friend. The Spanish girl wanted a home and lots of children. So for two years, I was "the other woman." We would meet on the roof of my forty-two-story building to watch the sunsets over the city skyline and share our deepest thoughts. He ended up marrying the Spanish girl; I had things to do, and he wanted to settle down. But we managed to remain good friends for many years, even after I moved away as an adult.

I think that chapter raised some self-doubt that maybe I was *too* ambitious and not the type to marry. Maybe I would never marry, I remember thinking. Self-doubt can trigger low self-esteem. I got a job so Mom and I could afford to live in the city. I applied at an Irish pub called Mumbles, on the corner of Ninety-first Street and Third Avenue. The two co-owners were family guys who came in only now and then but were very nice to me when they did. The bar's managers were friendly and fun.

I was still only fifteen, but I lied and said I was eighteen to get the job. It was years later that I learned the manager who hired me knew I wasn't eighteen but knew that my father had been murdered and that I needed to pay for my school and apartment, so he looked the other way and hired me.

The pay was $1.35 an hour, plus tips—and the tips were wonderful. I was always able to make $100 a day working Saturday and Sunday brunch shift. When I was sixteen, one of the regular Friday night girls was sick, so they let me fill in for her. The waitresses typically made $200 to $400 on Friday and Saturday nights. Although the restaurant was open till 2:00 AM, we didn't get out of there until almost four o'clock!

At the end of my first Friday shift, all the bartenders and other workers celebrated with me for a job well done. I felt so grown up, like a real part of the restaurant's family. It was me, Aurea ... I was able to work as an adult, making $400 a night at a nice Irish pub. I was able to make our co-op payment with one night's pay. *Look out Manhattan*, I thought, *Aurea is back!*

We had lived in Queens for only six months. It wasn't so bad, but it still wasn't home—Manhattan was. I had been forced to leave my expensive private school after ninth grade, due to my father's death. But now that I was working, I found a small private school for young professionals on the west side of the city that catered to young performers. I applied, and I was thrilled to be accepted. I began at the new school for the start of tenth grade, and then I took the accelerated plan to finish the eleventh and twelfth grades in one year, enabling myself to graduate at the age of sixteen, just three months before my seventeenth birthday—all while maintaining and A average in all my classes.

The teachers were great, and they tried to help those students who were capable of accelerating their learning process. I felt a real urgency to graduate quickly and enter the real world, where I wanted to attend Marymount Manhattan College—just twenty blocks from where we lived—and major in theater and dance.

I finished my freshman year at Marymount, then took a year off from college to focus on acting, I was accepted into the New York Academy of Theatrical Arts. I was attending the academy full-time and taking more acting and speech classes at the prestigious Herbert Bergdorf Studio in Greenwich Village, and I was paying for it all with my waitress job at Mumbles.

During my time at Herbert Bergdorf Studio, I auditioned for many things, like the movie *Hair* and my dream job at Disney World. Getting that entertainment job would have meant moving to sunny Florida and would have been a wonderful addition to any singer or dancer's resume. I kept getting callbacks into the audition room, until I was one of only a dozen applicants remaining in the dance line up. Once I knew another dancer was going to get it, I wished her well; she was amazing and deserved it.

Falling short on an audition never upset me, because I always gained experience and I always had fun. Being the cheerleader I was, I always rooted for everyone there to get the part, sometimes forgetting that I, too, was trying out for it. But cheering others on is something I've always done, and always will do.

After our return to Manhattan from Queens, I asked my brother and sister to move back in with us. But by then, they had their own lives unfolding, so they never did.

A lot of kids would have thought it a big deal to be supporting their mother, but I never thought twice about it. I would do anything to help my mother and me live in Manhattan. And I was learning to bounce, figuring out how to turn obstacles into stepping stones at a young age. And if you're focused on a goal, you will too.

10

Irish Coffee, Anyone?

Life at the Irish Pub was fun. I was working, going to school, and helping out at home. But to a teenager, it all just seemed like a big adventure.

Tommy Smothers from the Smothers Brothers used to come into the pub. He was always very quiet but very nice and a good tipper. There were lots of celebrities, too, and I always seemed to be bumping into them. In the city of dreams, they just seemed ordinary, just like me. But I always wondered how I could be more like them.

As a much younger waitress at the pub, there was a lot for me to learn. The other waitresses were older and much more experienced, so I did my best to learn from them. One day during a brunch shift, I was learning to balance a tray of Bloody Marys. The tables were close together, like everything else in the city. I took the tray to a table of six and lifted one glass. That was enough to spill one of the Bloody Marys all the way down the front of this guy's white polo shirt. He was super nice and just laughed, but I was so embarrassed. The pub did not charge me a cleaning bill or anything. But that was then. Nowadays, a spill like that often results in customers screaming and the restaurants deducting cleaning charges from the server's paycheck.

I guess at the time, they noticed I was young and nervous, so they were just great all around.

On one very busy day, an older lady called me over and pointed to her salad. "What is this?" she asked.

"It's your salad that comes with the meal," I replied.

"But what is this *on* my salad?" she shot back.

"Umm, the blue cheese dressing you ordered," I said, still not quite understanding where her line of questioning was headed.

"What is under the salad dressing?" she finally asked.

I looked closely at the salad and saw the little green grasshopper, covered in blue cheese dressing. Being the nature-lover that I am, I responded with the first thing that came to mind.

"Awwww, he's so cute."

The customer wasn't as amused, though, so I took the salad back to the kitchen and washed off the grasshopper, then took him outside and placed him gently under a tree. He hopped away happily, free from his salad dressing nightmare.

The lady at the table also survived, eating another salad that I prepared.

Yes, it was fun growing up fast in the city.

11

Prince Charming

When I was eighteen, I had my first real boyfriend ... Ah, young love. He was of German descent. He was my age and was from the group of friends I had hung out with at school. We went out to parties and fun things like that. Since this was my first real boyfriend, I thought it was normal for guys to be jealous of their girl-friends, and that I should be flattered. But he had a very bad, jealous temper. All his friends felt sorry for me because of the way he treated me. He would even kick me down the street during his fits of rage. But I had a boyfriend now, and that was better then being the other woman any day.

The relationship ended after a year because he found another girl, and I was crushed. Even though he was mean to me much of the time, he was still my boy-friend, and it made me feel pretty and important to have that in my life. Maybe it was a matter of bruised ego and hurt pride, but still I felt that I had lost some-thing, and I never liked the feeling of losing. It raised more self-doubt, that maybe there was something wrong with me. Why did they keep finding someone else? Wasn't I good enough, thin enough, or pretty enough? Maybe when I was rich and famous, I thought, I would have a wonderful and handsome man to live with happily ever after.

My mom saw that I was really depressed after my breakup with my boyfriend, whom she never liked because of his temper and possessiveness. After she saw me moping around for weeks, she came into my room and said, "Aurea, get up. Let's go to Columbia Pictures and get you a job on a soap opera."

Mom was working at Columbia Pictures at the time, and she knew a director. I started working on *The Edge of Night* with my brother. Doric even played the guitar and sang on several of the episodes. It was lots of fun, and I liked everyone and did well with the parts. The director liked me, and said he thought I had tal-ent enough to do comedy, too. It was the first time I was told that. At first it had been an adventure, but then I saw how people would virtually cut their best friend's throat to get a part. I was rapidly becoming depressed with rat race of show business and needed a break from it.

I knew I needed to finish college to get ahead. I loved animals and had even thought about being a veterinarian, among other childhood dreams. When I was in grade school, I had developed a passion for dolphins. Dolphins have been known to save swimmers in distress and were extremely smart mammals. I remember how Mom's German shepherd had saved me when I was a young child, and I believed animals were special. So at last, I traveled to Florida and saw my first dolphin in Busch Gardens in Tampa. I was so choked up that I had had tears running down my face. They were such amazing creatures. I knew right then that I wanted to work at Bush Gardens or Sea World.

My uncle Danny, Mom's brother, lived in Sarasota, and since I wanted to go to Florida so badly, I called to see if I could live with him for a month before the spring semester began at the end of February. Sarasota was just on the other side of the Sunshine Skyway Bridge from St. Petersburg and my new college.

I did not want to leave my mother in New York. Our Siberian husky, which we had since I was ten, had died, and the apartment felt lonely without him. Mother had started dating a man named Eric, whom I liked. After my mom and dad divorced, my mother had dated older rich men from her affluent social circle. These men were wealthy and could have given her the lifestyle she was accustomed to—but they typically bored her to tears as she dated for ten long years. Then one night, my mother went to hear one of her friends sing at Carnegie Hall, and I went to a party with my friends. I came home early that night because the party had been a bore, and I was tired. Mother had not wanted to go out that night because she was getting tired of the night life, but I urged her to go; I know God had a hand in that.

When I returned home to the apartment I saw a guy who looked like Tom Selleck, of *Magnum P.I.*, sitting on the couch. *Wow!* After I said hello and grabbed a snack from the kitchen, I went to my room and couldn't wait for him to leave, so I could hear the details of how Mom had met him. *Who was he?*

Apparently, he had also gone to hear my mother's friend sing at Carnegie Hall. The singer sent a limo for her friends after the concert. The limo was crowded, so the men sat on the seats and women had to sit in their laps. Mom had ended up in the cute guy's lap.

"I hope you don't mind sitting on my lap," he had said.

"How could I mind sitting on such a gorgeous lap," Mom replied, and away they went.

They were the last passengers to be taken home by the limo, and she realized that if she didn't do or say something, she may never see this man again. She thought quickly and invited him up for tea. He was only thirty and she was forty-five, but they were great together. She was five feet seven with long, blond hair and a great figure; she was full of energy and loved to laugh. Eric was six feet tall, dark, and handsome. He was an Italian artist from New Jersey, and within a few short years, they combined my mother's business skills with his talent and launched their own graphic design company. It was successful, and they made a lot of money and traveled all over.

I only knew Eric for a very short time before I realized that my mom was safe with him; I never would have moved to Florida and left her unless I knew she had someone special to take care of her. Eric had never been married and didn't have any children, and he treated me like I was his own child. I couldn't have asked for a better Prince Charming for my mom, and I prayed that one day I would find a man like him to be my own Prince Charming. I was so happy for my mother.

I left for my second year of college at the age of nineteen and tried to study marine biology, but my talent for show business overruled sitting in school all day. There were sunny beaches, auditions, and plenty of parties calling my name. After I moved to Florida, I dated a lot. I was blonde, tan, and only nineteen years old; all the boys found me fun and interesting, having come from the Big Apple. It was so exciting to live in a place where people drove their own cars everywhere, rode bikes to work, and played in the sand.

I dropped out of school for a while and got a job in an Oyster Bar as a cocktail waitress. It was there that I met my best friend, Lisa. Lisa worked in the gift shop, and we hit it off right away. The bar was a hangout for the college crowd and was also a hot spot for tourists. It was a great place to work. We were all like one big, happy family, and we made great money during tourist season.

The managers were also understanding about the fact that I had to have time off every six months to go spend time with my mother and Eric. I also had to go home for Christmas, because I couldn't imagine spending it without my mom in New York City.

My mother and Eric celebrating a New Year's Eve.

12

Jesus Loves Me

In Florida, I participated in several community theater plays, often in the lead role. My favorite was playing Bonnie in the Cole Porter musical *Anything Goes*.

When I received rave reviews in the newspapers, I was thrilled. Maybe I was a nobody in New York, but here I was recognized, and that was awesome.

I had always loved music, dancing, and acting. Laughter was on top of my list, too—I always tried to keep my sense of humor in any situation, so a waitress at my restaurant told me I should go to clown college, like her friend had done. After a little thought, I decided I would.

I graduated from Suncoast Classical Clowns with the name Crystal the Clown and clowned at a lot of auditoriums, parties, and fairs. I was in parades as a roller skating, white-faced clown, and even appeared as a featured clown in a comedy skit on the local broadcast of the Jerry Lewis Labor Day Telethon. I taught myself to juggle by using small teddy bears, and it worked. Making animal balloons and painting children's faces were my favorite parts of the act.

I once auditioned for the Burt Reynolds Theater in Jupiter, Florida, but in the meantime had a lead role in a musical at the St. Petersburg Little Theater. So many roles kept coming from that, so I stayed there.

Life was good in the sunbelt, and I began working at a spa teaching aerobics and running the front desk, While I was working there, I talked to a minister about my faith and was introduced to the Lord. After becoming a Christian, I had to leave the spa—people actually persecuted me because of my newfound faith. I was raised Protestant, because Mother had been raised in a Catholic school where the nuns beat her as a child growing up in the 1940s, so she no longer wanted anything to do with any church.

My salvation experience was personal, as is everyone's. Jesus saves each of us one at a time, and like fingerprints, no two salvations are alike. It seems Jesus will find you when you are at one of the lowest points in your life. Or more appropriately, we find him.

I dated lots of guys during this period in my life who took me to parties, movies, and amusement parks. It seemed that I was living just to seek entertainment, and I was becoming bored and discouraged. I asked myself where I was going. The guys I was dating had no ambition and seemed content living from paycheck to paycheck. They lived for Friday nights, when they could party and get drunk. The show business people were back-stabbers and would do anything for a part in a show. Even the girls I worked with at the spa were unfriendly, once I became a Christian.

My old back injury flared up again one night after I had stayed late to do the books. My back hurt so much, and I felt like crying. Our cleaning man came in with his twelve-year-old son. He liked to clean the spas at night for some extra money. He was a middle-aged guy who had strong muscles and a nice smile. He asked me what was wrong.

I told him my lower back hurt, and that I wouldn't be able to get home if it didn't get better quick. My old car was always breaking down and it was expensive to fix, and gas was expensive on my salary. So I had bought a bike for $5, and rode it almost twenty miles to work every day. I was young and enjoyed the rides, but on this night, I wasn't going to be able to ride it home; I was in too much pain.

The cleaning man said he knew someone who could help, so I got out my pencil and paper to write down the name of what I assumed would be his doctor.

"Jesus," he said.

Uh-oh, I thought. *This is one of those Jesus Freaks that I've heard about.*

But he said, "I love Jesus, and I know he can perform miracles, so can I pray for you?"

I told him he could, and so he prayed. I could hardly believe it when I instantly felt better; the pain was gone, and I felt as if some heavy burden had been lifted off my shoulders.

So every night for two weeks, I waited for this wonderful cleaning man to come to work and asked him hundreds of questions about Jesus and the Bible, and how God heard our prayers and answered it the moment we prayed. I was so excited that God answers prayer—sometimes immediately. So after two weeks of asking him questions, praying, and learning about a closer walk with Jesus, I gave my heart and soul to Jesus. I was born again on July 3. I did not go out drinking and partying on the Fourth of July that year, because I had found new life in the Lord.

He told me he was a minister and went to an nondenominational church, and so I began attending his little church and reading my Bible three or four hours a night, studying alone in my apartment with my dog, my cat, and my noisy bird. I talked to God in prayer every day now and found out how awesome He is, and I realized that the Bible is not just a good book, but the true word of God. And that the more time you spend in God's word and with him, the more you can hear His voice too.

This was far different from my nights of partying. I was learning to love to read as my grandmother had, and I was content and happy because I felt my life was now taking on purpose. I was feeling true joy in my heart, and it was wonderful and exciting.

Me in my Suncoast Classical clown costume, with my bright green wig on and holding my daughter, Angelica.

13

Days of Darkness

I like variety, and I was beginning to get burned out on being a waitress and bartending, The spa work was dull, but then I saw an ad in the local paper for dog groomers. It said I could make over $400 a week. Well, I loved dogs and had been very successful at age eleven as a dog sitter and dog walker, so why not a groomer?

I applied for and got the job, but they had neglected to tell me that the four-week training period was without pay. This was fine, because I knew the pay would be great once it started coming in. After my training period was over, they told me it was time to go out in the field.

"Can't I work here?" I asked. They said there were no openings in the shop, but maybe later—I would have to go out on a route for the time being. These were the days before MapQuest and onboard navigational systems, when one had to find directions by using a paper map or stopping at every gas station along the way to ask. I was new to driving, being from New York City, and I thought driving one of those cute little minivans couldn't be that hard. But when they drove the truck around for me, it was the size of a UPS truck, with no doors or seat belts.

I ran back into the shop. "You can't expect me to drive that! I've never driven a truck!" I gasped.

They all laughed at me and told me not to worry.

"You will be fine," they assured me. "Just call us from your first stop and we will tell you where your next stop is. Do that all day. Don't worry—piece of cake."

Right. Not to worry. So I got in the truck and began playing stop and go over to the beach area. I was lost and had to turn that sucker around. *Maybe it would be easier to cut through the Red Lobster parking lot instead of turning around in the road*, I thought.

KURCHUNK ... KURCHUNK ... KURCHUNK ...

What was that? I turned around and saw a clearance sign dangling in the breeze. I'm not used to driving a truck, and apparently I didn't have enough clearance.

When I arrived at my first appointment, I rang the doorbell and out came the biggest schnauzer I have ever seen! He weighed at least ninety-five pounds, and when he stood up and put his paws on my shoulders, he was taller than me. The bathtub in the truck was high up—how was I going to get this elephant up there? The schnauzer just seemed to smile.

I hoped he would just jump up there, but unfortunately, he didn't share my idea. I had to beg him to put one paw in at the time. It took me more than three hours to bathe that dog. They called from the office for the next appointment, but I didn't make it that day; it was too late.

As time went on, I gained experience and soon became a very good dog groomer. But my driving still left a little to be desired. The grooming jobs were typically long drives apart and they took a long time to do a good job, so I never did many dogs in a day; my pay was usually only $100 a week. Working in the salon was more lucrative, since time isn't wasted traveling. But unfortunately, that in-salon opening never came.

I still loved working with the animals, though, so when I saw a job opening in a pet store in the mall, I jumped at the chance. The store owner agreed to give me every Sunday off so I could attend church, which was amazing.

During one slow evening at the shop, I was standing by the front door, gazing out onto the mall area and watching people pass by, when I spotted a handsome guy. Our eyes met and we looked at each other for a moment, and we both seemed to recognize each other. He walked across the mall and introduced himself—very charming, I thought.

He shook my hand behind my pet store counter and introduced himself as Anthony (not his real name). We then realized we had seen each other just a few nights earlier in the grocery store, where we had kept meeting each other on every aisle. Finally, in the peanut butter and jelly aisle, he said, "We have to stop meeting like this."

I laughed and checked out, and didn't look back.

I had been a Christian now for a year, and had given up dating and partying to become a more mature adult. I was reading the Bible, trying to figure out God's plan for my life. So when this charming stranger introduced himself and said with no prompting that he was a Christian, that he was attended a nondenominational church, that his father was a minister, and that his family was Greek, it seemed too good to be true.

I had been praying to meet a Christian man. The fact that his father was a minister and that they spoke Greek had to be a Godsend. I had wanted to learn Greek because so much of the Bible was written in Greek. I had been brought up listening to a priest read the Bible, so reading it myself and actually knowing what Jesus had said was a thrill for me.

Meeting Anthony was not a case of love at first sight. But I was very attracted to him and figured he must know the Bible well and be a great Christian, since he was raised by a minister. I was only twenty-three at the time, and when I think back on the three short months we dated before we married, I was encouraged because of the fact that he was a good man from a good family. I overlooked his explosive temper and jealous streak that he exhibited right from the start. I guess I was shocked by his behavior, and that kept me from feeling that "in love" feeling. But I kept thinking he was the man for me—the element of him being a Christian from a Christian family was important to me—and I believed things would be better once we were married.

But I eventually learned that if a guy was abusive while dating you, it would be very unusual for him to change once you're married, and things will even most likely become worse. I know also now to observe how a man treats his mother—it's a window into how he will treat his wife.

After dating for a very short time, we were married. Greek weddings are supposed to be fun and merry. But mine was anything but that. His family argued over every wedding detail, and I felt that there was no pleasing anyone. I wore a hand-me-down dress from a friend at the pet store that wasn't even white—it was cream—since I was too broke to afford a new one. But this one fit, so I made it work. I appreciated my friend's generosity with the dress; her own marriage had ended in a bitter divorce, and she didn't like my fiancé. Nevertheless, she let me have the dress—I think because she felt sorry for me. My eager fiancé wanted to get married right away and did not want to wait until spring when Mom and Eric could have come down for the wedding. I later learned this broke my mother's heart, which in turn broke mine.

The minister who married us was the one who had led me to salvation while I was working at the health spa. We were married at the church Anthony's parents attended, with only a few people there for the ceremony. One of the sweet girls from my church was my maid of honor. But my new husband did not want me to have any contact with anyone from my past, so, my best friend in the world, Lisa, was not invited to the wedding. To Anthony, Lisa represented my wild past, and that was unacceptable to him.

I walked myself down the aisle, constantly mindful of how this was Eric's job and how my mother should have been there. I should have insisted we wait until Spring I thought, but he was too overpowering to me back then.

We had no honeymoon, and Anthony's mother came over to the house every day. I tried to be a good wife, doing my best to ignore his angry, jealous outbursts, truly believing that things would get better as time went on. But jealously has a way of taking over your whole world, like cancer—and it's just as destructive, slowly but surely eating away at your core.

To make matters worse, Anthony would constantly fire off angry and sarcastic remarks about guys looking at me.

"Why did you smile at that guy?" he would sneer as we passed some random person in the mall. After a while, I began to look at the ground at all times, so he wouldn't think I was flirting. His anger would last for days at a time.

The jealously worsened as the months rolled by. I wasn't allowed to wear sundresses with spaghetti straps, because my husband thought I was trying to flaunt my body to other men. Actually, I wore them because it's hot in Florida, and I was used to wearing cute dresses.

I couldn't understand why he didn't trust me; once I make a commitment, I am faithful, and he should have known that. He didn't even want me to take a walk by myself, because he imagined me running off with a construction worker that I might meet on the street. He would even inspect the gravel on the car tires to see if it matched the gravel at the place I told him I was going. He would check the car's mileage, too.

This mistrust soon spread to my job. He was afraid I might run off with a male customer who came into the pet store. So he made me quit and stay home.

This behavior does not make a woman feel loved. I became a prisoner in my own home. I missed work and had no friends, and all I had to do all day was cook and clean. He demanded everything to be perfect, but nothing was ever good enough for him. I was so lonely. I had always been surrounded by lots of friends and had always been very active. The first thing an abusive man does is separate his spouse from her friends and family and keep her isolated. Anthony even said he wanted to move out of town, so the neighbors couldn't hear him when he screamed at me.

I began to think a child would be nice; a baby would provide me with some company. I soon became pregnant with my daughter, and Anthony wanted me to avoid almost any contact with people other than his family. He came to the doctor's office with me for my first OB-GYN exam. To my horror, the doctor was a handsome young man, and kind of resembled a movie star. I knew I was in for trouble.

Sure enough, that night he accused me of liking the exam; he tried to make it sound like an erotic experience. He wouldn't even touch me for two weeks. So when we moved, he insisted upon a female doctor to deliver the baby.

We moved to Chevy Chase, Maryland, when he took a new job in his field. We lived there for two years, and I had my wonderful daughter, Dorea Angelica. The name means "angelic gift," and to me, that's exactly what she was. She was a huge blessing in my life.

In Chevy Chase, I could visit with my grandmother and talk to her about my faith. Grams was happy that I had married a preacher's son but had no idea how badly he treated me.

But I missed Florida so much! I had been glad to move to Maryland to be near my grandmother and to get away from Anthony's arguing relatives, who were at our house all the time. The television program *Everyone Loves Raymond* comes to mind in describing his family, but definitely without the comedic aspect of the show.

When I was twenty-six, we moved back to St. Petersburg. I missed Grams but loved Florida so much, even though we would have to live with his parents for a while. But it would be worth it to me to get back to my sunny Florida.

My husband allowed me to teach at the daycare of his parent's church. I taught the four-year-old class, and Angelica attended the two-year-old class. I loved being around the kids all day, and I could always make them laugh. I felt like I was not only working, but doing something for the Lord. I was even able to attend a community college and get my credits for studying early childhood development so I could earn more as a preschool teacher at the church.

But alas, my husband soon noticed that I was happy, so he decided there was not enough money in the daycare job and made me quit and go into sales at a local diet center. I knew there was no reason to cry, since crying wasn't going to help, so I bounced again and started to like the job and the people I worked with. I was helping people lose weight and feel better about themselves.

I had to meet with people all day, and so I thought I should look good. This led to my first—and only, thankfully—black eye, when I asked my husband for money to go to the beauty shop to have my hair done. We were in the car with our four-year-old daughter, who was awake in the back seat, and he punched me as hard as he could six times in my left eye. Thankfully, I didn't go blind, but later that day when I looked in the mirror, I was horrified at my disfigurement. He said it was my fault for making him angry, but then he tried to apologize. I still didn't think about leaving him, but I did think that having a little money of my own might not be such a bad idea.

So about two weeks later, I was sitting alone in my apartment, missing the world I once knew. I was still not allowed any contact with people outside of my job and the church, and I could have no outside interests at all. My husband had even made me give up clowning, and I missed the children and the parades terribly. I couldn't understand why my husband couldn't be proud of anything I did; I did things for *us*, not *me*, but he didn't see it that way.

One year before my daughter was old enough to go to kindergarten, Anthony said she could not go to private school.

"We have to pay taxes for public school, so that is where she will go," he declared.

"Over my dead body," I thought. I had private school all my life, and I wanted that for my one and only little girl, so I was willing to work to make that happen.

As I sat alone in our apartment while he was at work that day, God suddenly put an idea into my head. I heard his voice so clearly. It was one of those light bulb moments. He said for me to call this cosmetic company and find out how to earn the use of one of their company cars. Knowing God's voice is what happens when you spend time in his word and getting to know him on a daily basis.

I had told my mother about this cosmetic company I had heard about that offered the use of a company car to it's independent sale force. I had worked at the diet center for about a year, and my mother thought I would be a great businesswoman and wanted me to start the business. Mother had always thought I was beautiful, but I didn't think so. I was athletic and didn't care about cosmetics or frills. Mother said cosmetics were better than clown makeup, and selling them meant I could be my own boss.

So the next day, while my husband was at work, this lovely lady came over to my apartment and explained how I could earn the use of company cars and make lots of money if I worked at it. The lady, Mary Jones, said, "Hang onto my skirt, and I will take you to the top with me."

Wow! This sounded like a dream come true. My mother agreed and gave me the money I needed to get started.

After a year in the business, I had earned a company car to drive and put my daughter into a private Christian kindergarten, paid for with my new career money. I was making my own way again, and my self-esteem began to return. By 1992, I had earned one of the top positions in the independent sales force. I had secretly put money into my own personal bank account, which my husband knew nothing about. Every day, I came home from work, then did all the housework, took care of Angelica, did the laundry, had a home-cooked dinner on the table every night—no take-out or boxed meals for him, since he was used to his mother's home cooking from scratch. And, of course, he always let me know that my cooking would never compare with hers.

I worked until I was exhausted, still trying to be a perfect wife and mother. I had not been brought up in a home where there had been yelling and screaming and did not want my daughter raised this way.

So once again, in 1992, I bounced, and my life came around another bend and headed in another direction.

14

Prison Break!

I came home that day in my shiny new company car and parked it in our driveway. I had earned the use of it for a job well-done, and that made me feel wonderful. My self-esteem was beginning to grow like sap rising in a tree in the spring.

I was so happy with my new career and the ability to provide things for my child and contribute to more household bills then ever before. But my husband came in the door and immediately began yelling about how the windowsills were dirty. I could not believe it, since I had cleaned house most of the day. It was the last straw; seven years of screaming was all I could take.

I had talked to my mother on the telephone a few days earlier, and she told me, "Aurea, actions speak louder than words. Angelica is going to grow up and do exactly what you have done. You may tell her love is wonderful, but she is gong to think it is mean, jealous, and demanding. Love should be unselfish and giving, and not one-sided."

And Mother didn't even know the full extent of Anthony's abuse.

So instead of grabbing a cleaning cloth and proceeding to clean the windowsills, as I would have done in the past, I stood my ground and said "Get out!"

He didn't think I was serious at first, because I had never acted like this before. But when he realized I wasn't joking, he shoved me against a wall and called his mother.

"Mom come quick, Aurea is trying to leave me," he whined.

Then I noticed my little five-year-old daughter at the top of the stairs, with her Barbie suitcase packed. She was holding her teddy bear.

"I'm ready, Mommy," she said.

It was then that I realized my child was tired of the yelling and screaming too. She was tired of seeing her mother mistreated. Poor baby—she wanted out of this situation as badly as I did.

Anthony's mother arrived quickly, since she only lived three blocks away and brought with her a friend from church for backup. Now it was three against one.

"You can't do this to my son," she scolded. "You can't leave him."

There was so much commotion, and I was still pinned up against the wall, but then I had an idea.

"I need some fresh air to clear my head," I said.

I told my daughter to come with me for a quick ride. They tried to make me leave her, but I wouldn't. When that didn't work, they asked her to leave her suitcase. I told her to bring it.

"You will be back in a few minutes, right?" they asked me.

"Yes, I just want to take a ride. I'll be back soon."

I headed for the beach, which was only minutes away. As I drove, I knew they were going to look for me. I didn't want to bother my friends or make them lie for me, so I figured that if they didn't know where I was, then they wouldn't be lying when he asked them.

I thought about driving to a shelter for battered women that I had heard about on television, but I didn't know where the nearest one was, or even their phone number. So I drove to the beach and checked into a five-star hotel I was familiar with. We had our monthly fashion shows in that same hotel, so I felt safe in its familiar environment. It was expensive, but I called my mom and she said to stay there, and that she would come the next day. So I checked into the hotel. I took the big bow out of the back window of my car. If he drove around looking for me, he would surely recognize the car with a bow, announcing that I had earned the use of it.

We had a beautiful room on a top floor, and I cried all night. But my little girl was so strong and comforting. My mother arrived the next day, paid my bill, and went back to the house with me to confront him. We made him get out, and I filed for divorce. I let Mary, my cosmetic mentor, know where I was. She said there are no easy divorces. *No kidding!*

Anthony called me several times a day with threats and angry messages. Mom, my daughter, and I would have to leave the house just to escape the telephone harassment. He began to stalk me, standing across the street from my house, watching everything I did—and the restraining order didn't help much. My business suffered, since I could not even answer the telephone in fear of it being him, and I was under severe stress from all of it. My mother knew she would eventually have to return to New York, but she was afraid to leave me. She stayed for two months, with my stepfather's blessings.

Angelica asked if I was divorcing her daddy. I asked her what she would think about that, and she said, "Why don't you do it and get it over with? Daddy is always grumpy anyway."

It is amazing how perceptive and smart children are. She loved her daddy but wanted him to stop screaming at me.

My husband had never helped much with Angelica. He never changed diapers or gave her a bath. He acted like I had the baby all on my own and often told me that she was more my responsibility because she was a girl. I know I wanted the baby more than he did, but I never thought that he would treat us both so badly. I guess if things had been different, I would have had more children; I love kids. But God knew what was ahead for me and that there was another purpose in my life. So I only had Angelica, but she was definitely a blessing from heaven.

I asked God for help every day and prayed for the safety of my child and myself. I surrounded myself with friends and loving people and tried to do what made me happy. I began working at a dating club, thinking it would be a great new way to meet new people after being alone for so long. I became a wonderful matchmaker, and I loved helping make others' dreams come true.

But I was Christian and would never be unfaithful, so I would not accept a date until the day my divorce was final. When that day came, I had a date with a cute DJ I met. I felt pretty for the first time in seven years, so I knew more of my self-esteem was beginning to return.

My husband gave me very little weekly child support, and he would not have done even that if not for the courts requiring him to. I was too afraid of him to ask for more money. I should have let the courts handle it, because being a single parent was tougher than I thought. I had no idea the problems that I would face, and financially, we were soon drained. I had to ask churches for help, went to food closets, and even accepted food stamps for a while. I was divorced and still being abused, because now my ex-husband was saying he wanted to see me and my child starving in the streets. But I knew I was a survivor and a hard worker, and with God's help I would make a way for me and my daughter. I eventually was able to get the child support payment raised a little due to all the damage done to my business because of Anthony's harassment.

Mom and Eric were wonderful and offered me financial support for a while. Then Eric and my mom came up with the idea to have Eric legally adopt me, so I wouldn't have a last name I hated after the divorce and so that I could experience some much-needed happiness in my life. So at the age of thirty-three, I became Aurea Faltraco. I even acquired a new birth certificate.

As we sat in the judge's chambers, we conferred with a very nice judge. He asked Eric why he wanted to adopt me.

"I already love her as if she was my own daughter, and I would like for her to have my name," Eric said.

The judge then asked me why I wanted to be adopted, and I said with a smile, "Because I want to be Italian."

The judge, who was also Italian, laughed. "I can understand that," he said.

Then he signed the papers. It was a very happy moment in my life.

After my divorce, my mother found a great female counselor for me; she strongly believed it would help me, and she was right. I attended sessions with the counselor for a few months and soon realized that I didn't make my ex-husband the way he was. No matter what I did, the outcome would have been the same. If I had walked on coals or knelt before him, it would not have been good enough. The problem was in *him*, and he had probably come from a long line of abusers and seen his father mistreat his mother. I had no control over his actions, and no matter what I had done he would have never been nice to me. This was a good moment for me, as I began to release the guilt. I had tried so hard and felt that I had failed, but I had not failed. I was simply living in an impossible situation that would never have improved.

After years of abuse, I felt guilty spending money on myself for beauty products, at the beauty shop, or for babysitters so I could go out. Mom sensed the stress in my voice and asked me to send Angelica to stay with her and Eric in New York for a month during school's summer break, so I could have some time for myself. I could use some of the time to regroup and to get more work done to pay down the bills that kept mounting.

I couldn't bear the thought of sending my daughter on her first airplane ride by herself. But as I prayed for answers, I began to get a peace from God and felt it was the right thing to do. She was seven years old, and she stayed for a month, going shopping and to events with "Mommy two" and "Daddy two," as she called Mom and Eric. I joined them for the last ten days of her stay. We went shopping and to the Bronx Zoo, which was the first time I noticed my mother out of breath and tired—unusual for her. But I dismissed it, thinking that it was simply too much uphill walking and smoking, a habit that always had given her a cough.

I had the best time I had known in seven years. It was wonderful! My daughter and I flew back to Florida together, rejuvenated and ready to continue our single life. Everything seemed safe, just like the poem that Mother wrote when she was only twelve years old.

Stars

You must look up to see a star;
they lift your eyes and heart so far.
Above the world,
somewhere beyond a star, is God,
and gazing up it is not hard
to know that peace and love are safe
as long as the stars stay in their place.

Me and my official new dad, Eric.

15

A Healing Heart

I was working hard on my home-based business, all ready to earn the use of my second company car. We had been back from New York about three weeks, and Eric, my new daddy, called one afternoon.

I was glad to hear from him. I spoke to my mom every other day, but Eric wasn't always there when I called. But then he said the most horrible words, the ones you can't believe while hearing them. I will hear those words in my mind for the rest of my life.

"Sweetie, your mother has cancer again," he said. "This time, it is liver and lung cancer, and she has only around two months—or maybe just two weeks—to live, according to the doctors."

I was speechless; he had to be wrong. Mother had beaten cancer ten years earlier, and she was in New York City where all the latest in research and equipment is available. Michael Landon had just died from the same type of cancer a few months earlier, so I was scared.

My mentor, Mary Jones, had once been a nurse. She told me to fly to New York to say good-bye to Mom, because she would go quickly. I will be forever grateful to Mary for caring enough to tell me the truth. Mary made money off my earnings, but she loved me more as a person than a paycheck.

I flew to New York, not believing that Mom would die. This was a whole different type of cancer, different than the lymphoma she had ten years before. I stayed with her at the hospital for two weeks, and my brother came from California. Doric was very close to me during this time. He couldn't stay in New York as long as I did, but he and I would walk together back and forth from the hospital to the apartment every day—more than forty blocks each way. We'd eat at sidewalk cafes along the way and spot celebrities, just like old times. We had always loved spotting celebrities in the street growing up. We saw Marlon Brando eating in a café as we left the hospital, and O. J. Simpson was in the drug store, picking up a bottle of shampoo for me that I had dropped on the floor. It was before O. J. had gotten into all his legal trouble.

The last night before Doric left, he got out his guitar and sang to me. From the time I was just a tiny girl, he had always sung to me when I was sad, or before I went to bed at night. That night, I cried myself to sleep as he played softly sitting on the couch next to me. I cried for my mother, and because Doric was leaving the next day. I needed him so much.

The time came when I had to leave and go back to Florida and my daughter. I hated to go, but I told my mother I would see her on Christmas, which was only three months away. At Christmas, she was still alive but very weak, and she couldn't physically take the trip. I think I was still in denial, and believed she was going to make it.

Then at 4:00 AM on January 6, just eleven days before her sixtieth birthday, my daddy called and said in a choked up voice, "Honey, She didn't make it."

I couldn't talk, so I had to hang up the phone quickly. I then cried so hard, lying in my bed in the dark feeling all alone. I was so heartbroken; I felt like my heart was literally coming out of my chest. I physically hurt in my chest, like a heart attack, and I wasn't even sure I could go on living. Thank God I had my faith and my little girl to keep me strong.

It was two years before I could think of Mom and not cry while feeling like my chest was being ripped apart. But God never closes a door unless he opens a window. He never takes someone special home unless he leaves someone else to help us cope. I met Brian McGarry at the dating club where I was working on Nov. 27, 1993, almost two months before my mother died. I told her about him in one of our telephone conversations, about how we were going to see *The Nutcracker* ballet—my all-time favorite. I know my mother would have loved Brian.

On the day my mother died, I waited for a long time before calling Brian. I wanted to call him, but I had known him only a short time and felt a little uneasy about talking to him while I so choked up. But he was wonderful and sympathetic, and he told me to try to just remember the good times my mother and I had shared, and that she would want me to go on with my life and be happy. He had such a sweet sense of humor, and I did begin to feel better. But as soon as I hung up, I fell apart again. I'm so glad Brian was there, because it was a very long healing process, and Brian was up to the job.

After my divorce, I had drifted away from church a little, because working, dating, and caring for a child took so much time. I was mentally drained, and I did not want to continue going to his parents' church. But, I never lost my faith in God, and I continued to pray and seek His wisdom in my life. I still knew I had a greater purpose, as we all do, and I felt this so strong in my spirit.

I was constantly grieving for my mother; I had lost my best friend. I put my business on hold and waited tables for a while, and I continued working and managing the dating club. I was doing everything I could to pull myself out of my sorrow, but it was not working. Not yet.

About a month after my mom died, Eric called and wanted me to fly up to New York and help him go through her personal things. My boss at the dating club gladly gave me the time off. He was a great person, but he also knew that I always gave 200 percent to everything I did. It is just my way.

The day I had to leave Eric to go back to Florida was one of the saddest days of my life. I had several large bags containing items Eric said he knew my mother wanted me to have. I hugged him and said good-bye. When I walked onto the bus that would take me to the airport and looked back out the window at Eric's sad face, I completely lost it. Tears streamed uncontrolled down my face. The harsh reality that Mommy was gone and not standing there smiling at me with her arms around Eric, as usual, finally sank in. It was as if she had just died at that very moment.

As the bus drove away, I couldn't take my eyes off of Eric. He became smaller and smaller as we got farther away from that busy street corner. I was in New York without Mommy. How could New York go on without her? A New York without Mommy, to me, was like New York without Times Square or Broadway. I felt as if my soul had been ripped right out of my body. I was so weak I didn't know if I could get off the bus at the airport without falling to the ground.

At the airport I just stood there with my heavy bags. I couldn't get the attention of a sky cab or anyone—people were so busy. They had planes to catch and appointments to make. Didn't they know the world had stopped turning? Didn't they know it was the end of the world—my mommy was gone! I felt like the five-year-old girl in my dreams, running down dark halls in a theater looking for her. I wanted to call to her, but I knew she couldn't answer. She was gone, and it wasn't fair.

If only Brian was here, I thought. Maybe that was when I started realizing how much Brian meant to me. I had to drag my bags several blocks from the street to the check-in station, with tears still running down my face. My luggage was too heavy and began to tear at the bottoms where they were scraping along the pavement.

Weren't there any good Samaritans here today? Can anyone help me? But no one did. No one noticed my struggle. I think I lost faith in people that day for a split second. But people are only human; you can't put your faith in them. You have to put your faith in God and realize that He is our support system. He sees all, and He is my ultimate refuge in times of trouble.

Back home, on the first day back on the job, I was greeted by several of my clients who were surprised to see me. They had been told, by the girl filling in for me, that I was not coming back, which she knew was a lie. She wanted my job from the day she started, always talking badly about everyone behind their backs. She was known for her backstabbing ways during her short time with us. I had been home to help settle my mother's estate, crying on the streets of New York—and she was trying to steal my job. What kind of person would do that? The owner liked me. I was his manager and when he found out what she had done, he fired her on the spot. I hope she discovered that honesty and kindness are always the best policy.

Just surviving was hard. My paychecks were small, and my bills were large. I couldn't call Mommy for advice anymore. There were days during which depression almost got the best of me, but I knew God had a plan for my life—and maybe a man too. Was that man Brian?

I met Brian while managing the dating club in Tampa. I didn't want to date my own clients, so my friend that managed a dating club in St. Petersburg and I would visit each other's club. While at her club, I saw Brian's video. I thought he was gorgeous, with his blond hair, blue eyes, and tanned, muscular body. He had been a merchant marine and was an avid body builder, and he loved to roller blade, bicycle, and work out. He had also worked as an extra in television and movies, just as I had. We had so much in common.

Brian loved to tell stories about being a rigger on the *Bounty*, a ship anchored near his home in St. Petersburg, Florida. The ship sailed down to Mexico for several months at a time and while they were there, most of the crew worked as extras in the movies or for television. His favorite movie to work on was 1983's *Yellow Beard*, which featured the late Peter Boyle, and Cheech and Chong.

Brian also worked as an extra on *Indiana Jones* and on the television series *The A-Team*. Once while the cast and crew were all partying and having fun, Brian took the Lord's name in vain. Mr. T. was there and heard what Brian had said.

"Don't ever take the Lord's name in vain—*ever!*" Mr. T said firmly.

That made a good impression on a very young Brian, to think that a tough and successful guy like Mr. T had great respect for the Lord.

I had been an extra in a movie called *The Break* with Martin Sheen about a year before I met Brian, and we later figured out that we had both worked on the same set at about the same time. He was working behind the scenes while I was in scenes as an extra. We worked together on other movies as well and shared many of the same friends, but had never met for some reason. Apparently, it was just not in God's plan for us to meet yet.

Brian came from a wonderful, close-knit family in St. Petersburg. His parents have been happily married now for more than fifty-five years. His father is a retired circuit court judge, avid golfer, motorcyclist, and a very active man who loved to play badminton and teach it to kids at the YMCA.

Brian's mother, Norma Jean, was a stay-at-home mom who raised her two sons. She was a busy community and church volunteer, a philanthropist, and a devoted Christian person along with rest of their family. Her mother, Lucille, also gave generously to build a nurses station that bears her name at the children's hospital in St. Petersburg and funded a new fellowship hall at her church. Lucille's husband, Goodie—Brian's grandfather—loved children and people with all his heart. He was close to Brian and died only a few months before my mother did. I think that is why he was able to relate to my grief so well.

Brian's brother, Mark; Mark's wife, Susie; and their son, Patrick, live an active life. Mark is a district attorney and a top ranking cyclist in his states age division, Susie is a champion equestrian, and Patrick is a top-ranking BMX bike champion who ranked number one in Florida at age ten.

And I can't forget to mention uncle Joe, Norma Jean's brother, who always has time to listen and give encouraging words to Brian and I in all of our endeavors, telling us to "go for it!" in everything we do.

The entire family is so nice and warm hearted, and they have been heaven's gift to me.

The McGarry Family at our wedding garden party in 1996. From left to right: Brian's brother Mark, with wife Susie and son Patrick; Brian's parents, Norma Jean and Mark Senior; me, Brian, and Angelica in front.

16

My Knight

I had been dating Brian for two years and had my daughter in public school in Clearwater, Florida. I was constantly having car trouble; the brakes failed on one of my cars, and I had to run into a tree to make it stop. Thankfully, I had just let my daughter out to visit her father before that occurred, just two blocks from his house.

Another car of mine burst into flames as I was driving down the interstate in Tampa going to work. A woman on the interstate passed me frantically waving her arms yelling, "Your car is on fire!" I stopped, jumped out in my little short skirt and heels, and ran as far away from the car as I could. Two construction workers saw what was happening and ran with fire extinguishers to put out the fire. I was praying they didn't get killed if the car exploded. From the burned car, we salvaged my pair of roller skates, my basketball, and my box of materials from my career days in my cosmetic business.

That night, when Brian came to my apartment, he saw the box of career materials, burnt black like my dreams, sitting in the floor.

"Aurea, why did you give up your career? You said you enjoyed it," he said.

He looked up at my picture on the wall with the car I had earned the use of when I was married. "Aurea, you earned that car even while living in an abusive situation. Couldn't you do it again?"

"I don't have the money," I replied. "My mother helped me get started before. I don't have any credit because I had to file bankruptcy due to my financial salutation. I now have to make decisions such as, 'do I buy food or gas today?'"

"Enough of this car monkey business," he said. "I'm going to invest in your business and help you earn the use of another new car."

I had not spoken to Mary, my mentor, in more than a year—not since right after my mother died. But I called.

"Hi, it is Aurea," I said into the phone. "I hope you remember me because I want to earn another new car."

I was half-joking, but she said, "Aurea, I have never forgotten you; I think about you every day."

That gave me such a good feeling. It was like I was coming home to a warm place, a place where my mother knew I would be happy. Mother had loved this career for me, and Mary did, too. So now I was coming back to what I loved. No more food stamps for me.

Brian believed in me. He was always boosting my self-esteem, and he never put me down. He had faith in me, and he was so kind. And my daughter loved him. I couldn't help falling in love with him, although the first marriage had made me cautious of men. This was a man like Mother had found in Eric.

It was only two months after I had rejoined the world of entrepreneurs that Brian and I went to New York to visit Eric.

Brian proposed to me just minutes before the ball dropped in Times Square to usher in 1996. It was our second trip to New York. I had brought Brian the previous summer to meet Eric, and we had visited the World Trade Center Towers during that trip.

The ball was dropping—10 ... 9 ... 8 ... 7 ...—when Brian got down right in front of some ladies who were visiting from St. Petersburg (small world) and proposed to me—right in my favorite place in the whole world!

When all the shouting and party blowers went off and the confetti came down, it was if the whole world was cheering for us rather than the new year. We walked all over the city that night; who could ever have slept after that?

I was taking my mother's advice; I was going to marry my best friend.

17

Wedding Bells

Wedding bells were ringing, and this time my heart rang with them.

The only thing that could have made the day more perfect was if Mom could have been there, although I know she was. I could almost see her smiling down from heaven, and I knew she would be pleased to see I was wearing her white beaded gown that she had worn when she married Eric. He had wanted me to have it when she died, and I was so proud that I was slim enough to fit into it.

Eric had been there for her until the day she died, and this dress stood for that type of unconditional love. I know she would have loved Brian so much. It was February 11, 1996. Heart month—the month of love.

We kept the day we would say our wedding vows a secret, only because Brian was too shy to say them in front of a lot of people watching him. He was afraid he would make a mistake. So I honored his wishes, and we were married in our church by our pastor with Angelica as the flower girl. Then Brian called his family and told them. They were thrilled and threw us the biggest party on their gorgeous lawn with four hundred friends and a string band playing under their gazebo. This time, my "dad"—Eric—was there, and so was my best friend Lisa, with her husband Ron. At last, our friendship was rekindled. We will be best friends forever.

As a wedding present, Brian's family gave us a honeymoon in the Virgin Islands. We snorkeled so much while we were there, and Brian couldn't get me out of the water until after dark. It was like being in heaven. I had always wanted to learn to scuba dive, but snorkeling was the next best thing. I had always loved the ocean and sea creatures, like my dolphins. It was so beautiful under that clear, aqua-blue-green water—a whole new world under the sea.

In July 1996, I got back into my business and went straight to the top. With all of Brian's encouragement, and my daughter blossoming into a beautiful young lady, life was good. I had soon earned the use of another new car. I was a top recruiter with the company, because I wanted to tell other ladies about this wonderful business that had saved my life more than once.

After my battle with abuse, I loved helping women find the right cosmetics for them, and maybe the right business for them too. If you feel beautiful, you *are* beautiful. Beauty comes from the inside, and every woman wants to look her best. I feel like all women are sisters, and I love helping my sisters, inspiring them to be all that God wants them to be. I love to offer encouragement, and I hoped the love of God and the happiness I had found with Brian was radiating from me, so I could help others.

My birthstones for October are opal and tourmaline, which mean "hope." One way to pronounce my name correctly is to say "a ray of hope." But Brian always said, "a ray of sunshine." Either way, I want to give women hope. I want them to know they can bounce back, regardless of the obstacles. Others have gone before you, so hang on to the survivors for hope and encouragement.

Brian and me cutting our wedding cake at our wedding garden party.

18

Truffles Is Not Candy

We were happy, and my career was going well. Brian and I both loved animals so much, so we decided to reward ourselves with the gift of a pet for our first anniversary.

I had always wanted an umbrella cockatoo—big, white, gentle, and extremely smart birds. We found a breeder with some to sell and went to look at them one day.

While we were there, this amazing creature came out to greet us. It was a wallaby kangaroo. I was so excited. I had loved Skippy growing up, and here he was, in person.

Needless to say, we never looked at the birds; we were too mesmerized by this wonderful exotic animal in front of us. We purchased a smaller version of the wallaby species called a Damas kangaroo. She was only one pound, and we got her that following week. We bottle-fed her every three hours, just like a newborn, and named her Truffles. We carried her around with us everywhere we went in her own pillowcase. When she grew to full size—about fifteen pounds—she stayed home and played with our golden retriever, Scooter. Truffles would push celery sticks through the cage to Scooter, who would then walk around the house holding the celery stick in his mouth like a cigar. They were so cute playing together. She was so friendly and a wonderful animal.

Truffles would sit on the couch with us and watch television. She was truly a member of the family.

When we moved to Georgia, we were not allowed to keep her because it is against state laws in Georgia to have any wild animals as pets. Truffles was not wild, but the law could not be broken by anyone, and we were forced to give her up after raising her for five years. So after much investigating, we chose a wonderful place for her to live: the Dawsonville Kangaroo Conservatory here in Georgia, only an hour from our house.

It was a very emotional good-bye; I cried and cried. In her own way … I am sure she did too.

Our Damas kangaroo, Truffles, sitting on Brian's lap and snacking on one of her favorite things: oatmeal.

19

My Brother, My Hero

They say that life happens while you're making other plans, and that is so true. Brian had met Doric when he flew to the Florida Keys on a business trip. We drove down and joined him for the weekend, and Brian and Doric hit it off just as I knew they would.

Brian and I had been married for two years, and I had been telling Brian I would like to go to California to visit Doric because he had always been my hero growing up, and I knew he and Brian would get to be better buddies. But then horrible news came: my brother called me and told me that he had been diagnosed with cancer. Brian, Angelica, and I flew to California right away to support him through his first chemotherapy treatment.

I felt numb. Cancer had already taken my mother—*please God, not another victim so soon.* But Doric made it, just as my mother had after being diagnosed with lymphoma when she was forty-nine.

Doric had what they call the "Cadillac of cancers;" Hodgkin's lymphoma. Because it is curable. Doric was forty-two, and he made it through with flying colors. I was so happy and relieved and proud of him again; he always succeeded at everything.

Doric's chemotherapy and radiation were hard for him because he had always tried to take care of his health. Being a vegetarian and on a special health food diet for many years to protect his health, he was devastated at putting cancer drugs into his body, but his overall good health and strong body helped him to bounce back quickly and eventually run in a twenty-six-mile race for the Lymphoma Society. He raised more than $3,000 in donations and crossed the finish line himself, again making me so proud to say, "That's my brother!"

Doric finished chemo in the spring of 1999. I continued to work hard, helping ladies be beautiful and helping my young daughter, who was now back in private Christian school, to work on her voice lessons and get closer to achieving her dream of becoming a singer.

Life as a wife, mother, and successful entrepreneur was good. But God had an even bigger plan for my life.

20

Strike Three

Only a few months later, in September 1999, a pain kept burning in my chest. I even mentioned it to Doric earlier that year. He said that he didn't want to scare me, but told me his chest had hurt the same way before he was diagnosed with cancer, and he wanted me to have it checked out. I had a list of misdiagnoses from six doctors and two chiropractors, so my mother-in-law got me an appointment with a lung specialist, who ordered another round of chest x-rays.

"I'm going to be glowing with radiation from all of this," I thought.

The lung specialist also knew that a simple blood test to check my sedimentation rate would tell him what he needed to know. He was looking for inflammation that would indicate a problem or perhaps cancer, but he didn't say the "cancer" word to me yet. We made an appointment to come in for the results.

When the day came for the results, severe thunderstorms were raging outside—so bad that the schools and most of the businesses had closed for the day. I called the office and asked if the doctor was still seeing patients, and the nurse said the doctor still wanted me to come in. I should have known there was something strange about this.

When Brian and I got to the doctor's office, it was like a ghost town; only one receptionist was there. She took us back to the consultation room and when we sat down, she whispered to Brian, "I'm glad you are with her."

While we waited for the doctor to come in, I could see outside the huge glass window that the sky was turning a threatening black. When he came in, the doctor said my sedimentation rate indicates a problem, and there was a cloudy area in the x-rays that did not look good to him. A few tears rolled down my cheeks, despite the fact that I'm usually pretty good at holding them back. I wasn't sure whether I was crying because I was scared, or from the relief that someone had finally found something; I knew there was something there all along, but no one could ever find it before.

I'm sure Brian was nervous, but he held up well. A needle biopsy came next. That needle was huge—at least twelve inches—and to my amazement, it didn't show anything. They said it may have missed the mass in my chest, which at the time, didn't seem possible to me.

So now all they could do was perform exploratory surgery; this was a way to have a sure diagnosis. I was called away one morning from working a Zig Ziglar convention in Tampa, where former President Gerald Ford and many other powerful mentors were speaking that day. The doctor said he had me scheduled for surgery at 8:00 AM the next day, and that I had to get to his office as soon as possible for preparation work. I didn't want to leave the convention, and I did not want the surgery, but off I went.

On the way home from the convention, I thought about my mother. She had died so young, but I was even younger. I also thought about Doric, who also had been diagnosed with cancer but made it. As a Christian, I knew God would take care of me, but I didn't want to die. Who would take care of Angelica? How she would miss me! I still miss my mother so much. And then there was Brian. We had just begun our life together, and he needed me.

I had so many hopes and dreams, and all my life, my dreams either had been lost, detoured, or changed. Was I selfish for wanting to live? Everything seemed surreal, as if I was living a dream. I tried to think about the past, and I tried to visualize the future. But for once, everything was frozen in the moment. Was this it? Was I going to die?

I felt very cold. Florida is a warm place, but I felt as cold as ice and as empty as a bucket with a hole in it. But I believed in God's healing power and knew to hold tight to his word as we took this next step together.

I went with Brian and his parents that day to sign release papers and my living will. The doctors told me a heart specialist would be doing the surgery since the mass was so close to my heart, and they planned on removing all of the mass they could. They would test it during the surgery, and remove it if it was cancerous. I had to sign permission for them to remove whatever they needed to.

Needless to say, the night before surgery was the longest night of my life. I prayed, and in a small way, I thought I knew how Jesus must have felt the night before his crucifixion. He had prayed, "Father, please let this cup pass from me." He didn't want to die, either, but he knew it was God's plan. That is why He had come into the world: to die so that we might live, and to give us a chance to pray for healing too.

Was I going to die? Would I ever come out of that operating room alive? I could almost picture my funeral, with Angelica and Brian crying, but I stopped myself. I chose to speak life into my body and continue quoting the scripture that tells us, in Isaiah 53:5, *"By his stripes we are healed."* I claimed it with all my heart and soul.

At 5:00 AM, I was up and ready—at least as ready as I ever would be. The sun was not even up yet, and the phone rang. I thought, "I am dreaming; none of this is real. It can't be happening."

I answered the phone; it was a very successful woman in our company who had just returned from an important sales convention in Switzerland. She told me she and the entire company were praying for me. Wow! All the women who I looked up to and admired were praying for me? I felt a warmth go down my spine, just knowing at that moment, heaven was being bombarded with prayers for me. I hope Katherine knew how much that call meant to me.

Then I remembered what I had to do. God knew what was going on, and he had a plan. It was time for me to stop trying to figure it all out and just ask God to proceed with his plan for my life. He was the potter, I was the clay. I had a peace.

Okay, operating room, here comes Aurea.

At the hospital, Angelica gave me a small stuffed camel from her McDonald's Aladdin collection. It was her favorite animal, and she wanted it to keep me company during surgery. I remember camels had come to Jesus's birth, too, so I guess they are pretty honored animals.

Everyone came to visit me at the hospital: all of Brian's family, my pastor, Mary Jones, Lisa, Brian's prayer partners. I felt so loved. I laughed and joked with them until it came time to roll me down the hall into the operating room. I felt tears flowing from my eyes that I could not stop. I was going somewhere I had never been, and none of my family could come with me. I had to walk this lonesome valley, but Jesus was there with me, holding my hand. But I am human, and for a few moments, the flesh gave way to a fear of the unknown.

I tried to control the tears rolling down my face. I wanted to be strong for my daughter; I didn't want her to see me cry.

Then I woke up in the ICU about four hours later with tubes coming out of my throat and chest. I still had Angelica's camel in my hands. I later learned that the doctors had put it back into my hands after surgery.

There was a woman standing at the foot of my bed praying. She was praying out loud with her hands up in the air toward Heaven. She was a part of our company's independent sales force. She had heard I was having surgery that day, and she had been to five hospitals until she found the one I was in. Although she wasn't supposed to be in the intensive care unit, she had found a way because

God told her to come and pray with me. She was a woman of great faith and with a mission, and I thank her for being faithful to it. I never did see her again, but it was a good feeling to know someone was there praying out loud over me. It was like a warm bath, giving me a feeling of peace as I awoke from surgery.

The doctor came in and began explaining what had happened during surgery. As I listened to him speak, I heard God whisper in my heart so clearly at that very moment: "You will write a book that will inspire others." So I was faithful to his words.

On October 7, 1999, I was diagnosed with non-Hodgkin's lymphoma. It was my birthday. I couldn't help recalling that my real dad had died on his birthday. Whatever happened to happy birthdays, anyway?

I know Brian saved my life because he took me to the emergency room for chest pains in the middle of the night, and then to six different doctors that entire year. All the other doctors just thought the pains stemmed from old sports injuries, and one doctor even assured me that the pain was not life-threatening, or I would have been dead already—his exact words.

But Brian was determined to help me find the real cause for this horrible pain that would not go away. His mother finally asked me to see a lung specialist friend of hers, and the exploratory surgery was eventually performed.

The McGarry family was wonderful to me and checked on me constantly. They are like my own family and are such a blessing. They stuck with me through the whole ordeal right by my bedside everyday, and I am so blessed to have them in my life.

21

Will I Ever Speak Again?

"Cancer" must be the most awful word in the human vocabulary. I had already heard its sentence pronounced on both my mother and brother, and now it was my turn. I had faith, but when they said that word, I felt like someone had taken a knife and ripped my guts out.

I knew from the start that the pain in my chest wasn't normal, and I never believed it was related to a sports injury. I knew I had injured the disks in my back when I tried to help move the furniture during our move from Manhattan to Queens, but this was a constant ache that made it hard to breath, and I always felt tired and out of breath.

The autumn leaves were falling; it was such a beautiful time of year. I always loved October, my birth month. But I knew my locks of hair would soon be falling with the red and gold leaves.

I was in severe pain after the surgery. They had removed my thymus, half of my left lung and a portion of my right lung, the lining around my heart, and the left thoracic nerve to my vocal cord. They also had to disconnect half of my diaphragm. They told me I would never speak above a whisper again.

Speaking, of course, was a big part of my life. I used the telephone to motivate, train, and take orders, so being unable to speak would be a big problem.

"God, please heal me so that I can speak, or help me to learn how to do my job and live my life without speaking," I prayed.

Either way, I would give God the glory. I would have to take my new life one day at a time. This was all new territory for me, but I was up for the challenge, and I had faith that God had a plan for me.

For a year I was unable to speak above a faint whisper, but then I did speak and it was a miracle, because now I speak much louder than a whisper. I am unable to sing or shout, but God is good, and miracles happen when all the facts say it is impossible. God wanted me to help others by being a motivational speaker, and I do that now better then ever.

I worried about Angelica. How would she take this? She would be starting high school next year, and to have her mother sick and not being there for her would be difficult. Teenage girls need their mother very much, and I didn't want to miss out on this crucial part of her life. She later told me that she had not been worried, because she knew I had so much faith in God's healing power, and she had faith in it, too.

She knew I would be fine, and I never saw her shed a tear.

22

Chemo Stinks!

In November 1999, I began chemotherapy. I had heard people got very sick while undergoing chemotherapy, but no one could have prepared me for that experience. My body was already ravaged and sick from so much surgery, and it really hadn't had time to heal. But it was important to start chemo treatments as soon as possible.

I was so sick I could not even stand up. I vomited, sweated, chilled, lost weight, and felt as though I was dying. But I knew I wouldn't die; God had brought me this far, and He wasn't going to leave me now. I had a peace about that.

I listened to the entire Bible on my compact disc player because the steriod caused my eyesight to be blurry most of the time. My hair and eyelashes fell out. I also ballooned from the steroids, gaining thirty pounds after the treatments were over. I didn't want to look in the mirror.

Most people at my doctor's office were only sick a day or two after their chemo treatments, but I would be deathly ill for ten straight days with no relief. I was unable to eat, or stand for very long, and I could barely walk to the bathroom. I threw up eighteen times a day, and would lose ten pounds overnight because my stomach was rejecting the drugs. I felt like I was a hundred years old.

The doctors had to put me in the hospital for five days after every chemo treatment, replenishing my fluids intravenously. They said I was one of the sickest patients they had ever seen on chemotherapy.

It seemed like my chemo treatments were taking an eternity, but it was only from November 1999 through February 2000. A few months of pure torture and having to force myself to have the strength for each treatment. The worst part was that after two weeks of being so sick following a treatment, I would start to feel like I might live again—and then it would be time to do it all over. I was so tired and weak.

Brian and Angelica were there throughout the ordeal, loving and supporting me. They told me I was beautiful, even when I could not look at myself in the mirror. Brian would rub my back and my bald head, even for hours at a time, to keep my mind off of the pain in my body. There was a constant pain in my stomach. But God was there, too, saying, "You are going to make it through the storm and the fire."

So I held God's word in my heart, and I knew he was keeping me alive for some very special reason. I saw God's blessings everywhere, including another miracle that happened during this experience: I received a visit to my hospital room from my former in-laws—Anthony's parents. Carrying a huge stuffed animal in their arms for me, they came over to my bedside, prayed for me, and told me how truly sorry they were for all of the past and how much they really did love me. I received a similar sentiment from Anthony himself over the phone that same week. We are all on great terms now with no hard feelings. The past happened for a reason.

"Out of severe circumstances can come great things and great healings. All things work together for good to those who love God and are called according to His purpose" (Rom. 8:28).

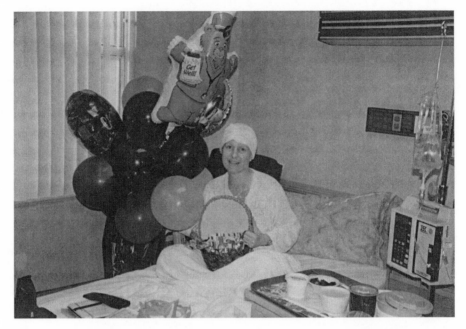

Me in the hospital recovering from my final chemotherapy treatment. I was still promoting all the new spring colors of cosmetics to all the nurses, who helped me so much in taking my mind off of being sick.

23

Cancer-free!

It was New Year's Eve 1999, hours away from the year 2000; the old year was fast dying. I was hardly able to sit up and see the fireworks only three blocks from our house. I couldn't walk through the grocery store without feeling like I was going to pass out. I felt like the year 1999, like I was quickly fading away.

But, no, this was going to be 2000—a new millennium, a new life, and a new beginning for me. I was determined to make it. I was going the find the reason God had led me to this.

Yes, yes, Lord, I thought. *I'll say yes to your purpose. I will make it. I will tell others what you have done in my life. I will enter the new millennium singing your praises. You have let me live, and I will live for you!*

I would lay on the bathroom floor sick for hours and pray. "Please Lord, don't let my suffering be in vain. Please help me to use my pain for good to help others when I make it through this."

When a person experiences cancer in their body, it changes their entire outlook on life. I began to appreciate every day that I just woke up. I loved meeting cancer survivors and hearing their stories. It was great to see them active after the battle. I looked at old people and thought, "Wow, they made it."

I don't mind growing old; it would mean I had made it, too, that I was alive. But I didn't really want to *look* old, so my cosmetics help with that.

My first-year checkup after the chemotherapy was great, and the doctor told me two years was a milestone for non-Hodgkin's lymphomas; if you make it two years without it returning, it's a milestone. Five years without it returning, he said, usually meant it would never return. When lymphomas do come back, they are usually worse the second time around. Thanks to the new drug Rituxon, which I would receive two days before each chemo treatment, the relapses in patients are dwindling down each year.

The first and second checkups were the most nerve-racking. I got to know the nurses and doctors at Gulf Coast Oncology, as well as Dr. Knipe and his associates. They were all so nice to me. Things actually got to the point that I looked forward to seeing them—but not to the complete blood test, full-body CAT scan, and iodine injection (for contrast). I have small, hard-to-find veins, and they usually had to poke me five or six times to find a good one. Ouch!

I made them take my port out after my last chemo treatment, although they recommended keeping it in for a year, just in case. But I knew I wasn't going to need it, so I acted on faith and had that thing removed.

24

Road to Atlanta

In June 2005, I was given the great news: I had been cancer-free for five years! We had a party to celebrate, and we were so happy.

I badly wanted to be my usual athletic self again, but every time I tried to ride my bike a few miles, I would suffer immobilizing chest pains. The steroids had put thirty pounds on me in only two months after my last chemo treatments. Exercise made it difficult to breathe; the doctors figured scar tissue was the likely culprit and assured me it would get better in time.

I kept trying, but to no avail. I really needed a physical therapist to work with me, but I couldn't find any who specialized in patients who had undergone chemo, or had organs removed.

To this day, I still struggle with my weight. I can no longer overeat and expect to work it off tomorrow—it just doesn't work that way for me anymore, now that vigorous exercise is such a challenge. I have yet to find a workout that doesn't cause physical chest pain for weeks afterward. But I miss being athletic, and I hope to one day be able to exercise and bicycle long distances again.

Only five months after my last chemo treatment, in August 2000, my family and I were able to buy our dream home, near Atlanta, Georgia. We wanted this so my daughter could pursue her singing career in a place with more opportunities for her. At first, I felt too weak to move our entire life to another state, but God somehow gave me the strength.

The new house was four thousand square feet larger than our last home and had two huge sets of stairs in it. I was in no shape to climb these stairs every day. I began to indulge in a little self-pity.

I have half of both lungs missing, half of my diaphragm not pumping air, no muscle tone from having been in bed for so long, and, thanks to those steroids, an extra thirty pounds, and now I'm supposed to climb stairs?

But it ended up being the best therapy possible for me. I climbed those stairs thirty times a day, unpacking in our new home. Every week, I improved, becoming less and less out of breath. I tried to walk the hills in our neighborhood, but senior citizens passed me like I was standing still. But I kept at it, and soon, I was moving faster.

The hills were alive, but not with the sound of music—rather, with sounds of heavy breathing and cries for help as the chest pains from the scar tissue would force me to stop.

But at least I had the stairs—it was a start.

25

Mrs. U.S. Beauty of Georgia

It was August 2000 when we moved to Georgia, and by January 2003, I had to get serious about dieting, since exercise was hard for me. I limited my carbohydrate intake to approximately fifty-five grams a day.

I learned that my body stores carbohydrates, and when I drop them down, my body began to lose weight. Yes, the weight was going—hooray!

I began to feel like myself again, and after one of my close friends was crowned Mrs. Florida, I wondered what would happen if I ran for Mrs. U.S. Beauty Georgia of 2003. I knew if I placed, it would help other women know that it is not all about being a size two. I wanted to enter the contest to reach more women and inspire them that we are *all* beautiful. I wanted them to know that beauty is about the *whole* woman, inside and out. You don't have to be skinny as long as you feel good and keep a great attitude in life; beauty is not about size and shape.

I wanted them to see that hair, lashes, and muscle all return, but if they don't, that's okay too. But most importantly, I wanted to make them realize that beauty comes from character, and character comes from making it through life's challenges.

Through my whole ordeal, I never lost my faith in God, nor my sense of humor. I had goals: I had to see my daughter grow up, and I had to grow old with my wonderful husband, Brian. And now I was working at my cosmetic business again, making a huge success of it. Every day, I was showing women how beautiful they were—they just had to look beneath the surface to recognize it.

I won Mrs. U.S. Beauty of Georgia and was named first runner-up at the national contest. I also was named the most photogenic contestant, and my favorite trophy that night was for the most inspirational contestant of 2003. I wore my crown with pride, and it was just another confirmation that God did indeed have a plan for my life.

To this day, I enjoy judging beauty contests that have a purpose. Some pageants teach young girls about community service and how they can start making a difference at a young age. One seventeen-year-old I met in my work for Relay For Life started her own beauty pageant to help find cures for cancer. She was president of her own company even before she graduated from high school. The winners of her contest all donate time to hospitals and do year-round fundraising.

What a wonderful purpose that girl has found for her life. My hat is off to everyone who participates in any events like that.

Brian posing with me as I wear my winning crown as Mrs. U.S. Beauty of
Georgia 2003.

26

Change: A Fact of Life

By this time, Angelica's singing career was beginning to take off. She is very talented as well as very beautiful, and our move to Atlanta was partly to advance her career.

She auditioned for the second season of *American Idol* at the age of sixteen, and was called back three times that week until she made it to the final day of the auditions. Because we were in business for ourselves, Brian and I were able to go with to her each day of the audition. She was called back for the final audition to sing in front of the three famous judges. Some of the girls were leaving in tears, but the judges were very nice to Angelica and told her she was very good, but not quite ready—but they thought she should come back next year.

Unfortunately, the following year, life had started to change for my daughter. She lost focus on her dreams for a while, and I pray that one day it will return. She has such a beautiful voice, and people loved her when she sang in various Atlanta nightspots. But she was young and in high school, and she could not keep late-night gigs. After her high school graduation, however, our lives changed once more.

It was 2004, and Brian and I had been to Florida for my annual checkup with the oncologist. The news from the doctor was once again good, and I was ecstatic. "Cancer-free" has such a beautiful sound!

We came home to Georgia about 10:00 PM. We had left Angelica at home to watch the house and care for the dogs. She was now eighteen and a very responsible young woman who was a lot of help to us.

As we came into the driveway, we noticed the garage door was open, and our John Deere lawnmower was not in its place in the garage. Little did we know, as we were about to enter the back door, that our lives were about to change forever—again.

We were greeted by my daughter and her new boyfriend, whose name I would like to forget. They acted casual, as though everything was cool.

"Where is the lawnmower?" I asked.

"Oh, it's down the hill in the back yard," Angelica replied.

"Why is it there?"

"Well, we had this way cool party last night," she explained. "We wanted to have a bonfire, so we drove the mower down to use its headlights to light up the yard while we chopped down a couple of trees for the fire."

"You what?!" I bellowed as I grabbed a chair to keep from fainting. The expression on Brian's face told me this wasn't going to be good.

"What on earth could you kids be thinking?" Brian yelled. "In this subdivision, you have to have a permit to do anything—like cut down trees. And bonfires are definitely not permitted!"

I thought Brian was going to have a stroke, a heart attack, or maybe both. He took one look at that boy, pointed his finger at him and said, "You drive my mower back into the garage into the exact spot it was, now!"

The boy said, "Oh, I would have put it back, but the battery is dead from running the lights so long."

"Jump-start it and get it back up here, now!" repeated Brian, who was now the color of a ripe tomato.

"Oh, my beautiful trees. They were so lovely, and now they are only stumps in the ground," I cried.

"Wow, Mom, I didn't know you loved trees so much," my daughter said.

I was in shock. How could this conversation be taking place? Did I have to make a not-to-do list for an eighteen-year-old that included things like "Do not party," "Do not run down the battery on the mower," "Do not chop down any trees," and "Do not burn down the subdivision while I am away"? This was unusual behavior for her and was the result of hanging with new friends who showed her new behaviors.

That was in October 2004, and it was not until May 2005—on Mother's Day—that my daughter told me that she was pregnant, which I figured out was as a result of that infamous party. Angelica's pregnancy had not shown, and when I found out, she was due in about six weeks. My sweet, talented daughter was pregnant by a boy who treated her worse than my ex-husband ever treated me. But she was in love, and she didn't recognize the abuse.

Love is blind, and sometimes deaf and dumb, too. Having lived in an abusive situation, I could relate to her feelings. Sometimes the woman feels she is partly to blame—but why?

I spent countless hours in tears during those long two years they were together, as I lived out a mother's nightmare. I watched Angelica spiral down this familiar road, headed for despair, and it hurt so much worse to watch my child go through it than when it had happened to me. Thankfully, they are no longer together.

God always turns things around for good for those who love him. It was true again in this situation. After I thought I was totally drained to the core, another miracle arrived in the midst of all this mayhem.

It was June 24, 2005, when my sweet granddaughter Alyssa Brooke was born. She had huge, dark blue eyes and brown hair, and she smiled on that first day by dinner time while she was in her Grandpa Brian's arms. She immediately became our newest love, and I knew my life would never again be the same. But changes are good, and are all part of life. Wheeeeeee! Back on the roller coaster of life we went.

Alyssa was so wonderful—a little miracle. But Angelica was young and not yet ready for the full-time responsibilities of motherhood. She was still in an unhealthy relationship that would consume her for another year-and-a-half. My husband and I stepped in and gained legal guardianship of our precious granddaughter.

So after seeing my daughter graduate from high school, and thinking our school years were over and that we were free to pursue our lives and careers, life took another turn, and parenthood began all over again for me—and for my husband, who never had a baby of his own. But we learned that other grandparents were doing the same thing. Thousands of them, willing to share stories and offer advice. We have gone to support meetings in our area, and they are easy to find in your local paper or online.

So no matter what your situation is or what you are going through, you are not alone. Someone has been there and done that, and even has the T-shirt to prove it. My T-shirt collection was getting much larger. But my life was full; I truly cherished every moment of every day.

Life never stops changing, and thank God that He has a plan for all of this. My daughter is now dating a mature young man who we like a lot, and who treats her like the wonderful young lady she is.

One day, Angelica will be able to step into the role of full-time motherhood. She loves her little girl so much. But until then, we will make sure our granddaughter has a great life with us. Alyssa loves to sing and dance, just like her mother and me. She is the light at the end of what was a very long, dark tunnel.

I'm building memories every day, and someday when I am gone, these memories will be all my family will have left of me. I don't want them to remember me being sad, angry, stressed, or too busy to notice them. I work and play like there is no tomorrow. It cures procrastination. And really, how do we know? Just because a person doesn't have cancer doesn't mean they are guaranteed a tomorrow.

How many people went to work on September 11, 2001, having any idea that it would be their last day on Earth? But many of those families directly affected by that terrible day had their last phone calls from their doomed loved ones, telling them of their love. Some families will always remember their loved ones' heroic actions of battling the terrorists aboard United Flight 93—actions that caused the plane to crash and prevent it from killing others by slamming into another building.

Moments like these are what take our breath away, and these are the moments that shape our lives. Who ever would have thought I would have so much happen in my life? What will be next? I am excited to see what will be next, because I know that with God's help, we can do all things. I will enjoy the journey.

My daughter, Angelica, at age 18.

My granddaughter Alyssa at age 2.

27

God's Plan for Your Life

One of the most helpful things for me—and maybe for you—is to surround yourself with encouraging, happy people. Negative people can bring you down and short-circuit your self-esteem. Choose to be positive instead.

Life is like a roller coaster ride and is filled with problems. But what truly matters is how we handle the cards we are dealt. You can be positive, have a good attitude, and learn to bounce. Never lose hope.

Have you ever noticed an ant? He carries over one hundred times more than his weight on his back. How does he do it? Well, no one ever told him he couldn't.

You may recall the story of the ant who thought he could move a rubber tree plant. He never heard the word "can't," and "oops, there goes that rubber tree plant." Then there's the bumblebee. Aerodynamically, a bumblebee should not be able to fly, because its wings are too small for its body. And yet, it flies.

You can fly, too. We all meet with challenges and broken dreams. But that doesn't mean we should stop dreaming.

There was once a play on Broadway called *A Raisin in the Sun*. In this play, the star had lost his dream, and he asks, "What happens to a dream deferred? Does it dry up like a raisin in the sun, or fester like a sore and run?"

Yes, something happens to a dream deferred. But don't let it dry up like a raisin in the sun. If you dwell on it and become bitter, it will fester like a sore and run. Be positive. Think of what part of the dream you can salvage and go with it; change is what life is made of. Maybe you always wanted to be a foreign missionary but couldn't take the required shots due to your health or found learning foreign language too difficult. But think of all the children now in America from other lands—you could be a home missionary.

Perhaps you dreamed of being a psychologist but couldn't afford graduate school. There are children in the public school system who need a counselor, so how about being their saving grace? Or suppose you went to acting school with a dream of staring on Broadway, and it hasn't happened yet. There's always the Little Theater, or the possibility of starting a theater company in your own home town.

You know you are a great photographer, but for whatever reason, your photos still have not made it into *National Geographic*. Couldn't you teach photography in a community college, or as an entrepreneur, in the meantime?

Suppose you want to be a mother and it has not happened yet. So many motherless children in the world need you, while you stand in faith on having your own someday.

I could go on and on. Sometimes a dream gets redirected, so keep your eyes and heart open while you continue to strive for your ultimate goal. Consider enjoying what you love in different ways as you continue to climb toward your ultimate summit. Life is a journey not a destination, and you should enjoy the trip along the way and not spend your days being unhappy until your ultimate dream comes true. God can use you along the way, too, as you enjoy using your gifts and talents on a daily basis.

What is God's plan for your life? If you seek it, I believe you will find it.

28

Finding Your Purpose

Are you happy with the way your life is unfolding? Is this where you thought you would be at this stage in your life? Is something holding you back? Are you merely existing, or are you *living*? If you answered "existing," why?

We are all like that little piece of clay that has to be molded by the potter's hand, put through the fire, and then painted before we realize our true purpose. Do you remember that story of the little tea cup? She didn't know her purpose until she was fired, painted, and filled with the warm tea—and then she was content.

My purpose is to help you find *your* purpose and thrive through your life's journey, and that is what we will be doing in the rest of the book. Sit back, read, absorb, and then act. Your life is waiting!

There are so many encouraging words out there for those who want to go forward. Women, I can hear you roar, but I love this poem so much, and it is so true of women in general, so I wanted to share it with you. Enjoy.

One Flaw In Women
Author unknown

By the time the Lord made woman,
He was into his sixth day of working overtime.
An angel appeared and said,
"Why are you spending so much time on this one?"
And the Lord answered, "Have you seen my spec sheet on her?
She has to be completely washable, but not plastic,
have over 200 movable parts, all replaceable,
and be able to run on diet soda and leftovers,
have a lap that can hold four children at one time,

have a kiss that can cure anything from a scraped knee to a broken
    heart,
and she will do everything
with only two hands."

The angel was astounded at the requirements.
"Only two hands!? No way!"
And that's just on the standard model?
That's too much work for one day.
Wait until tomorrow to finish."
But I won't," the Lord protested.
"I am so close to finishing this creation that is so close to my own
    heart.
She already heals herself when she is sick
AND can work 18-hour days."
The angel moved closer and touched the woman.
"But you have made her so soft, Lord."
"She is soft," the Lord agreed.
"but I have also made her tough.

You have no idea what she can endure or accomplish."

"Will she be able to think?" asked the angel.

The Lord replied, "Not only will she be able to think,
she will be able to reason and negotiate."
The angel then noticed something,
and reaching out, touched the woman's cheek.
"Oops, it looks like you have a leak in this model.
I told you that you were trying to put too much into this one."
"That's not a leak," the Lord corrected.

"That's a tear!"
"What's the tear for?" the angel asked.
The Lord said, "The tear is her way of expressing her joy,
her sorrow, her pain, her disappointment, her love,

her loneliness, her grief, and her pride."
The angel was impressed.
"You are a genius, Lord.
You thought of everything!
Woman is truly amazing."
And she is!
Women have strengths that amaze men.
They bear hardships and they carry burdens,
but they hold happiness, love, and joy.
They smile when they want to scream.
They sing when they want to cry.
They cry when they are happy
and laugh when they are nervous.
They fight for what they believe in.
They stand up to injustice.
They don't take "no" for an answer
when they believe there is a better solution.
They go without so their family can have.
They go to the doctor with a frightened friend.
They love unconditionally.
They cry when their children excel
and cheer when their friends get awards.
They are happy when they hear about
a birth or a wedding.
Their hearts break when a friend dies.
They grieve at the loss of a family member,
yet they are strong when they think there is no strength left.
They know that a hug and a kiss
can heal a broken heart.
Women come in all shapes, sizes, and colors.
They'll drive, fly, walk, run, or e-mail you,
to show how much they care about you.
The heart of a woman is what makes the world keep turning.

They bring joy, hope, and love.
They have compassion and ideals.
They give moral support to their family and friends.
Women have vital things to say and everything to give.
However, if there is one flaw in women, it is that they forget their worth.

My granddaughter Alyssa is a new light in my life now. She is walking, talking, smiling, singing, and dancing. She has truly been a blessing from God. She makes us laugh and smile everyday. I hope Alyssa and Angelica read this poem often and take those words to heart. Women are so special in so many ways, and we need to be reminded of that daily.

I have found that life is a series of events that we either make the best of or let get the best of us. And through all of its ups and downs, faith, love, laughter, friends, and dancing—in your heart and with your feet—all somehow help us feel better as we grow and learn through each and every event that comes our way.

I hope you all keep on dancing.

Granddaughter Alyssa and me—she will call me "Mommy Two."

My daughter Angelica and me.

29

You Can Do It!

Are you dancing? I hope you are free of abuse and dancing, or if you are ill and not able to dance right now, I hope you are dancing in your heart and spirit.

Or perhaps you are not ready to dance yet. If not, then on to the next two parts of my book: to lay out a roadmap for you to follow to overcome what is holding you down, so you can survive to thrive. I believe it was not an accident that you chose to read this book today.

Either you or someone you love may be in an abusive situation, or has a life-threatening illness. If it is not you, but a loved one, then do everything within your power—and with the help of God—to help them overcome their situation.

We all need a support system, and you can be part of someone's support system. Don't push or nag, but let them lean on you. And then, I hope you lean on God and praise Him in the good times and especially in the rough times. "Therefore by Him let us continually offer the sacrifice of praise to God, that is, the fruit of our lips, giving thanks to His name" (Heb. 13:15). It is a true sacrifice of praise when you do it when you don't feel like it, when things are at their worst, and you still lift up your voice to praise Him and all His goodness.

PART II
Escaping Abuse

In Part 1 of this book, you have read the story of my life so far. As you can see, I am neither a saint nor an angel, but a very real woman … just like you or the women around you, if you are a man reading this book. I have had my share of struggles to overcome, and although your struggles may not be like mine, they are just as important to you, because they are your problems; everyone has them.

The old saying is that you are either starting a crisis, in the middle of a crisis, or coming out of a crisis. We must learn to deal with our problems and move on, to keep thriving despite them, and refuse to stop chasing our dreams until the crisis has subsided. Life keeps happening while we are making other plans. There is no time like the present to make changes to improve your life and the lives of your loved ones. You can handle whatever comes your way, even if it takes a village to help you. It may be difficult, and even devastating, but God will help you too, if you let him.

I am neither a doctor nor a psychologist, so sharing the wisdom I have gained through my own struggles is intended only to inspire you to seek out whatever remedies work for you. I pray that sharing my stories of how I handled each situation—and how God helped me through it all—will provide a ray of hope to you and help you realize that whatever you're going through may be part of your legacy in some way. I think sharing our life lessons helps make all of our bad and challenging times a little easier, just by knowing we can help someone else who may be facing similar situations. Realizing that some roads are much harder than others, but that they have been traveled and survived by many, should inspire everyone to know they can make it, too.

In April 2007, I was listening to the morning news while I dressed for the day. My ears perked up when a segment dealing with domestic violence began. I watched as statistics flashed across the screen: in the United States, three women are killed by their husbands or boyfriends every day; three million women a year are abused, and that number increases every year. It was a number that was disgraceful; I couldn't believe it.

I want to do my part to reverse the upward trend of these statistics. I think we need to begin with education, with classes as early as elementary school, teaching children what is acceptable and unacceptable treatment of their fellow humans. It should be instilled in young girls that violence is not acceptable and that love is not supposed to hurt you. If violence is already occurring in their homes, they may be accepting it as a way of life. Is this becoming a country where we have no respect for life, especially of those we supposedly love? We must start changing the world now, one child at a time. Maybe by the time I am a great-grandmother, we will see a difference. I hope so, and I will do my part the best I can. Will you help too?

As an abused woman, I lost my self-respect and had low self-esteem for a long time. If not for my faith and my child, I might have also lost my will to live. I managed to escape abuse and find another life, and you can, too. But first, you must want change, have a goal, and create your own plan to reach that goal. My words in these chapters are for both women *and* men—I am not so naive as to believe that men are not sometimes abused by women too—although you will find that my words speak toward women because I am a woman and that is where my experience is coming from. My passion and my ministry is to help empower women to be the best they can be, but both sexes please take heed. The words in this book may touch the heart of the special women in your life, and that may be the reason you are reading it right now, so you can give it as a gift to enrich them.

My brother, Doric George, is a therapist in California, and he e-mailed me these words of wisdom one day after I asked him a few questions about domestic abuse. Here is his quote:

> "Let me say that I did not know you were being abused, Aurea. I knew you had a restraining order against him, but I thought it was for harassment. Mother never told us anything. It is typical for an abused woman to try to hide the abuse, so I'm not surprised that you didn't tell us. If my daughter was being abused, I would start by trying to get her to realize that she was *being* abused. Denial is the hardest thing to overcome, and you also have to want out of the situation. Once she wanted out, I would help her to *get* out. How I would do that would depend on how she got into the relationship, my relationship with the guy, and whether I had noticed it going on. I would have to discuss it with her mother. Maybe we would have to set boundaries or engage professionals. If she were living with the guy at the time, I would have to catch him in the act or help convince her to move out. Lastly, I know I couldn't do anything alone. I would engage everyone I could in the process. It could look a lot like an addiction intervention."

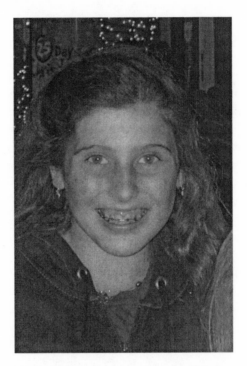

Doric's daughter, Jasmine—my beautiful niece.

My brother's words carry a lot of weight; he has studied and worked in the field of domestic violence during his career. How about you? Are you in denial? Are you being hurt? Are you ready to move forward? Here are some of the many things I have learned along the way from experience, from being counseled, from seeking God's wisdom in His powerful word, and from spending many years with other women across this country who have gone through this cycle of domestic violence and have come out of it on top. Again, you must find what works for you. Here are just a few things that have helped me.

1. How do you recognize abuse? Some women think their spouse is only controlling, or that it is his right to mistreat them. I believe you are abused if someone is constantly tearing down your self-esteem verbally.

I have heard that it takes eleven positive things to be said to a person to counteract one negative remark. Sometimes we think that if the abuse is not physical, it isn't so bad. I used to think that, too. I only had one black eye, but it took two weeks for my face to go from black to blue to red to purple, and then back to white. But the seven years of verbally tearing me down and screaming at me constantly took a much longer recovery time.

I had to surround myself with many positive people, including a new man in my life. As adults, we have choices of whom we allow into our own private space. Change is not easy. Decide whether you are in a relationship that is good for you, and whether, if you have children, you're sowing positive seeds into their lives. Is your home a happy place that makes you feel good about yourself? Do you feel safe? Do you and your spouse "complete" each other? Do you cheer each other on in your pursuits of your hopes and dreams? Do you truly want each other to succeed? Are you best friends? I don't believe that best friends would ever tear each other down with degrading names and constantly scream at each other in a hateful manner.

No one is perfect, and everyone argues sometimes. But there is a difference between arguing over legitimate problems and being awful to someone on a regular basis. I think that type of behavior needs to be dealt with.

Abuse can also come from employers, co-workers, and various others in your life. I can't believe it when some women tell me they are degraded daily by their bosses. I can't help but think, "Don't they know they are dependent on their workers, and their own success depends on a happy, motivated staff?" It is not a smart move to treat your employees like that. Life is too short to be stepped on day after day, and it is sad to hate going to work every morning.

2. Do you feel you deserve this treatment? If so, why? No one deserves to be abused. You must change your attitude. Steps toward a change in attitude begin with doing things you really enjoy.

Starting my own business and having use of a company car was a real self-esteem boost for me. My success gave me a sense of accomplishment, and positive recognition boosted my self-esteem, even though I didn't immediately realize it. I went into business because I needed a car and more money, and I needed to change the direction of my life. The happier you are with yourself and the more you use your God-given talents, the better you will feel, and you will be less tolerant of people pushing you around.

If you do not recognize your talents, think about what you like to do; your talents lie in the things you love. God gave you abilities, but he needs your availability in order to use them for good. He will take it from there. I wasn't very adept at selling when I entered that field, but God saw me venture out, He blessed me, and I earned as I learned—and discovered talents I never knew I had.

3. Does your husband or boyfriend want to change? Do you love him enough to help him change? Do you really *want* to change? If so, then seeking counseling is a great way to go. I am not a psychologist, but I believe couples counseling is good. And from my experience, so is individual counseling, during which a person can work on their individual problems and concerns. Christian counseling is often available through the church at no cost, or perhaps just talking with a pastor will do the trick. You should go to God daily in prayer and seek his wisdom as well. I know God was my saving grace and my help in time of trouble. Because as it says in Matthew 19:26, "with God all things are possible."

4. Are you tired of the abuse and want out? There are lots of people and organizations that can help. But you must take the first step. The Internet and people you know can help you find support groups or counselors. You can also read other books like this one to learn ways other people have escaped abuse. Prayer, family, friends, self-help literature, church, seminars, and counseling are just a few resources that have helped me with my journey, and they can help you, too.

If you are low on funds, or are in a scary situation, you can call the National Domestic Violence Hotline at 1-800-799-SAFE, and go to my Web site to see more resources available to you: aureamcgarry.com

5. You need to be clearing your head and rebuilding your self-esteem. You might feel like you are on the boxing ring canvas, down for the count, but don't give up. Fight! You can be a winner and recapture your self-respect by simply taking a long look in the mirror.

Who do you see? Are you the same person you were a year ago, or even a few months ago? Do you recognize yourself? I went into cosmetics because I wanted to help people look good. When you look good, you feel good. Poor appearance is one of the first signs of low self-esteem. Keep up your morale and appearance.

What about those extra pounds? Or have you lost so much weight that you look ill? Remember that regular exercise, fresh air, and fruits and veggies are refreshing to your body. You should stay away from junk food. Yes, every woman needs that once-a-month chocolate splurge. But if you want to be *really* good, there are sugar-free chocolates available, and they are delicious, too.

Maybe you are on a tight budget, but a new hairstyle, a new outfit, a manicure, and some makeup can perk you up, too. These gifts to yourself don't have to be expensive. Consignment stores even sell cute clothes, and maybe a friend would help with a manicure or a new hairstyle. It doesn't have to be radical; just a little change is good, and it complements the change taking place inside of you.

Don't even go the grocery store without makeup. You may look fine without it, but don't you usually smile at yourself in the mirror after you apply your lipstick? That's it ... smile! It takes fewer muscles to smile than it does to frown, and will cause fewer wrinkles. So smile at everyone you meet today. Even though your heart may be breaking, do it anyway. Most of your smiles will be returned, and I bet your heart will lift—at least a little.

6. Build a support system and surround yourself with encouraging, positive people. You tend to mimic the people closest to you, so choose those people wisely. No man is an island, and neither is a woman; you need your friends and family to help you now, so let them.

My dad, Eric, had this to say to me about my abuse:

"When your mother and I found out you were being abused, jokingly she said she wanted to shoot him, and I was ready to supply the bullets. Your mother said, 'No one has ever hit my little girl before and they are not going to start now.' She vowed to get you safely out of that situation, and she did."

Also, figure out something you have always wanted to do—a new hobby, career, or special adventure—and do it. My new business has given me several new, positive friends and glamorous gifts through out the years, but my self-esteem was the greatest present of all. It is rewarding to earn prizes and pick up keys to a new car that's yours to use for two years, and then you earn another one for a job well done.

But that rewarding feeling doesn't apply only to cars. It applies to anything big you want to accomplish. We are all given talents, and it is a shame when they aren't tapped. I know I have not even come close to achieving all God has in store for me. I will keep striving and going forward until the day I die, because it's not over until it is over. I want to accomplish everything God wants me to, and this is the only life I've got, so it is now or never. I know one thing for sure: I will never quit, give up, or stop striving, because the effort is up to me—the results are up to God.

7. Forgiveness is an important part of your healing process. There are many times while Anthony was harassing me that I felt hatred toward him; that was normal. But to heal, I had to let that go. I had to release all my negative feelings toward him and everything that had happened to move on with my life.

I focused on the good that had come from my bad marriage. There was my daughter, Angelica, and now my beautiful grandchild, Alyssa—those were the best results. Also, by living through the abuse, I am now in a position to help others in an abusive situation, and the Lord seems to be leading me every day to someone who needs that type of help and encouragement. Jesus had to become human in order to fully understand our needs, and as an abused woman, I fully understand yours.

When Jesus was nailed to the cross, he said, "Father, forgive them, for they do not know what they do" (Luke 23:34). Perhaps a verbally abusive spouse also does not understand the permanent scars they are giving their partner with cruel, degrading words. You must get away from dangerous abuse, but then practice forgiveness. Go to the Lord in prayer and ask him how to forgive, and He will help you. You also must forgive yourself. If you had bad feelings or actions due to the abuse, forgive yourself and seek God's forgiveness for that or anything that may have happened as a result of that abuse, and then move forward. Let the police handle any violence or other criminal acts, which need to be reported immediately. Never seek revenge. "Vengeance is mine, I will repay" (Rom. 12:19).

If we seek revenge, it only furthers the violence cycle. Only when we have been to the Lord in prayer and cleaned our hearts and minds do we understand forgiveness. You have made it through someone's intent to harm you, and now you have new power. You will carry a deeper compassion for those who suffer. You are changing. Now imagine the person you would like to become, and work to become that person.

Many people are aware of global warming, and they read about how we could change the world. But they think, "Well, maybe we could change the world, but not in my lifetime, so why should I try?" We can achieve a lot in our lifetimes. What if our forefathers had not sacrificed? Where would we be? It is not all what we will achieve in this lifetime, but what we die trying to achieve, and what we teach our children as we pass the torch on to them.

Someday our great-great-great-grandchildren may know a peaceful world without violence, but that peace must begin in our homes. It must begin in our hearts. Saving the environment must also begin in the homes as we learn not to waste and want so much. The Bible says, "When I was a child, I spoke as a child, I understood as a child, I thought as a child; But when I became a man, I put away childish things" (1 Cor. 13:11). As we mature, we can rise above jealousy, hatred, and abuse; it is a choice we can make. I forgave my sister for her mischief as a child, because she was just that: a small child. She grew and matured, and we became close friends during our teenage years before she moved out. She first moved to Texas, and later to California, where she now lives. She grew up to earn her college degree and thrive.

8. Keeping a journal of your life and progress is great therapy and a great release of your inner thoughts, but keep it well hidden. While growing up, I had kept a journal of all the poems I had written, pictures of my party days and old boyfriends, and the like. But the night before I married Anthony, he and his mother found my journal and threw it away while I was at work. He thought he was throwing away my past and all my memories. He didn't understand that every part of our lives come together to make us who we are. We learn from our failures and our triumphs. I wish I still had my poems, writings, and pictures to leave to my children. I have enjoyed going through all of my grandmother's old writings, some of which date back to 1914, when she was only eleven years old. I'm so glad no one threw them away, because now I have them to hold on to, and it makes it seem as if she is still right here with me.

9. Figure out what you need to be happy. You need to enjoy life, at least most of the time. When you have worked hard and come out on top, it's a great feeling. But if you are not enjoying the lifestyle you dreamed of, than make the decision to make yourself happy. Today is the first day of the rest of your life, and tomorrow could be too late. Ask yourself what would make you happy—or at least happier.

Is it a new career, a promotion, a new relationship, or working on your present relationship? Is it a wild adventure, photography, painting, or volunteer work? Read about the subjects that would make you happy; readers become leaders. I hope that reading my story gives you that ray of hope that you need to go forward and dream again. There *is* a light at the end of every tunnel, so keep a good attitude.

And it is okay to cry. That is a release, so let it out. Then let God help you move on and learn. There is a reason for whatever is happening, even if you don't understand it now. Believe it, and don't give up.

10. What is standing is your way of accomplishing these goals? The most common obstacle that stands in people's way is fear. We have a saying in our business that fear is simply "false evidence appearing real."

"Anxiety in the heart of man causes depression, but an encouraging word makes it glad" (Prov. 12:25).

When I was in my bad marriage, I remained in it because of fear. Fear of change, fear of the unknown, fear of my baby girl losing her daddy, fear of being alone, fear that all men were just like him, fear of failure. Lots of fear. I was young and inexperienced at the time, but life educated me along the way. Do not let fear stand in the way of becoming all you can be. You will be afraid, but feel the fear and do it anyway. Remember the Twenty-third Psalm: "The Lord is my shepherd … Though I walk through the valley of the shadow of death, I will fear no evil, for you are with me; Your rod and Your staff, they comfort me." Step out in faith to make this world a better place because you have lived here. What will your legacy be?

11. Staying focused on your goals is also important. I have learned so many ways to stay focused on goals from the inspiring, courageous women I work with. We all freely share ideas, and that is such a blessing. I would not have accomplished anything without the constant encouragement and teaching from my company and the amazing sales force, and especially from my business mentor, Mary Jones. Mary is one of the many successful entrepreneurs in our company. She taught me how to make posters and helped me to stay focused on my dreams. She says, "Aurea, you can't stand still. You will either be going forward, or you will be going backward. Standing still is losing ground and momentum on what you are trying to accomplish."

Make your own goal posters. They can be many sizes and hung all over your home or office. I teach my team to make 8 ½" x 11" posters. Do the front and back, and then laminate it. Punch a hole in the top corner and use it as a key ring. It can hit you in the knee while you are driving to constantly remind you of your goals. If it is big enough, someone will ask you about it, and you will have to tell them some of your goals. And it will be a constant confirmation to yourself that you are going to achieve your goals, because what you think about and speak about comes about.

What should you put on your goal poster? It should be filled with pictures of what you want to accomplish. It should have due dates written on it. To be a goal, it must have a date, otherwise it still is just a dream. The date will make you get butterflies in your stomach because it is scary enough to make you stretch yourself and your belief barriers. But it should not be so simple that it is easily accomplished and doesn't stretch you.

You can take your big goals and cut them into small segments. As you accomplish each segment, it brings you closer to the whole and the end result. I have daily, weekly, monthly, quarterly, and yearly goals. I also have goals that are two or three years out there, such as putting money away to start a nonprofit organization, buying a vacation home, and taking a big family vacation in Switzerland. So be sure to have some big goals along with the smaller ones. Whatever you want—whether it is a new car, a new house, or getting out of an abusive situation—determine what it will take to accomplish it and start working towards it.

Remember, "someday" is not a day of the week. Your goals should be so important to you that nothing will distract you from working to reach them. I wanted private school for my daughter more then anything else in the world, and I needed a new car. At the time, it wasn't only a want, but a *need*, and I couldn't work as if it was all right not to accomplish these things. So my goal of acquiring those two things kept me going and achieving. Giving up was never an option, and setbacks were just obstacles—things to go over, under, around, or through.

Mary always said, "You can judge the size of a woman by the size of the obstacle it takes to stop her." That kept me going every step of the way. Plan your goals and work on them every day. Work as if there is no tomorrow, because you just never know—someday, there won't be.

12. Congratulate yourself, you are at step twelve. You have come a long way, baby, and there's no turning back now. Do something to reward yourself. Perhaps an evening out? A spa treatment, maybe? A softening facial and dynamic glamour makeover?

Rewarding yourself will give you the energy and excitement to continue reaching for your big goals. All work and no play can be self-defeating, so take time out to go to a sporting event, get a massage, go dancing, have a date with your sweetie, or just relax in a bubble bath. No matter what, pamper yourself—you deserve it! But don't rest on your laurels, either. Get back up the next day and plan the big celebration you will have when you reach your ultimate goal.

How will you feel then? Who will you celebrate with? Never lose sight of your big day. I am planning the day I reach the top of my business and the debut I will have with my family and friends. I get tears in my eyes just thinking about that moment on stage. It keeps me going through the tough times, because I visualize the party I am going to have when I reach the top and the thousands of lives I have helped change along the way. Feel the joy, and it will come to pass. But you have to work for it. Hard work is good for you; it builds character, just like tough times do.

13. You are human, and there will be setbacks, but get back up, dust yourself off, and start all over again. No excuses!

Remember when you were learning to ride a bicycle? You no doubt fell off a few times. Well, you will have a few falls, but don't let them discourage you. God is with you. Don't beat yourself up for having a setback. Just start again. Rome wasn't built in a day, and you won't reach your goals in one day, either. Take one step back, then take two steps forward.

You have heard them all before. Now take them to heart.

14. Like a person with an addiction, I have seen victims of abuse sometimes slip back into an abusive situation. I believe that staying in professional counseling a good length of time is always a good idea to help avoid this; how long is different for everyone. Everyone heals and recovers from obstacles at different speeds, so there is no single, clear answer. Know that God is not finished with us yet, so keep the positive influences in your life flowing. And cut the negative ones out.

Don't give up. If you are out of your bad situation, be very careful about a new partner or relationship. Date this person long enough to see if they show any signs of extreme abuse. If so, run from this situation.

When you are really interested in someone, you may want to tell them about your bad experience and tell them you refuse to ever be in a situation like that again. Confess out loud to yourself and others that you are important and deserve respect, because you give respect. If you have stayed with an abusive partner who is trying to change, stay in church and in counseling, and don't stop just because things have improved a little. Go to God every day in prayer and remember that love can change things. So love God, your family, and yourself. Joy can be spelled Jesus, Others, You.

Also, take care of yourself physically, mentally, and spiritually, and work on your goals while always setting new ones. Stay busy and interested in life. Make friends, share activities with your children, and help others who have been in your situation.

15. How do you see yourself ten years from now? How close are you to achieving your dream? What will you do to ensure you realize your dream?

I was watching television one Sunday night, channel surfing around and looking for the weather to see how bad the cold front moving in was going to be, when I stumbled on to one of my favorite preachers: Joel Osteen. I was tempted to stay on that channel and watch, but I thought, "No, I had better just find the weather and go to bed … it is so late."

I found the weather channel, but they weren't giving the local forecast, so I switched back to Pastor Osteen. I wasn't in the mood for anything intense, since it was very late, but God is so good. Pastor Osteen was talking about giving birth to your dreams. He talked about how his mother had been diagnosed with terminal cancer twenty-five years earlier, and how she refused to give up. There she sat, in the front row, alive, well, and beautiful. A miracle.

Then he shared a story about a woman who had asked God for a baby twenty-nine years earlier, and she kept planning her nursery and talking every day about how she would soon need to take maternity leave. Then one day, twenty-nine years later, she learned from her doctors that she was pregnant with twins. She never gave up her dream. I can imagine the discouraging things that were said to her during those twenty-nine years.

Are you that passionate about your dream? Are you willing to refuse to give up, even if your dream takes twenty-nine years to come true?

Then I started thinking about my lost dreams. There were so many times I heard those nagging little voices inside my head tell me that I wasn't good enough in my career, because if I was, I would be in the very top position by now. I have worked hard for more than ten years, and anyone can make it to the top in our company. Success is not for the chosen few, but for the few who choose to be successful; it is not an appointed position. "I guess everyone else can make it, but maybe I wasn't meant for that high of a position," I thought. "I have accomplished a lot in my career and am in the top 2 percent, so why try any harder? Where I am is very impressive."

These are all self-defeating thoughts. I bet you have them, too. Well, I'm not going to let them win, and you shouldn't, either. When I hear about people keeping the faith for twenty-nine years, it inspires me. They realized their dream, and so can I. And so can you.

I know women who have made it to the top of our company in less time than I, who are breaking records every year. I could easily become discouraged, if I let myself. But I thank God that I tuned in to an inspirational message that night. It was if that message was meant to kick-start my dreams all over again.

We all need that from time to time. I believe my calling is to keep working through all the obstacles, so when I do get to the coveted, top position in my career, it will be a great day for me, my family, and my friends. I want people to hear my story and realize that what matters is not where you start, or how long it takes, but that you finish the good race or die trying. Dying while in motion is better than dying with hopes and dreams lying dormant that will die with you. When—not "if"—I arrive at the top of my career, I will set a new, loftier goal. I'll say "Where to now, Lord?"

I can't wait, because the day I die I want to have been busy doing something worthwhile, still filled with faith, dreams, hope, goals, and plans for the future.

16. Everything you have been through and overcome has made you stronger, and you need to keep going forward, full speed. Get up every morning and begin the day with prayer and praise. Ask the Lord to help you through this new day he has given you and to help you make the right decisions. Shower in the morning with revitalizing shower gels—they will wake you up. Try some perfumed body lotion, powder, or a little cologne to make the day smell better. Eat a healthy breakfast—cereal, fruit, juice, vitamins—or have a protein shake. Get organized and determine how much you can accomplish today.

Don't try to overdo, but go to work, run your errands, delegate housework, and always keep working toward your goals. Don't let yourself become too stressed. Sure, there is heavy, aggravating traffic slowing you down, but fuming won't help. Instead, pop in a CD of peaceful music or an uplifting motivational speaker. Call your best friend on the cell phone, laugh ... and what's that on your key chain? Ahh, your goals! Read over them again, and know you're going to make it.

And don't skip lunch; it is your energy and fuel. Make time for a brisk walk or some exercise, have a nice dinner, and try to get six to eight hours of real sleep. Live only one day at a time. You are working towards your goals, so accomplish a little bit each day. And always believe that you are going to make it. These things have helped me so much.

17. By now, perhaps you have achieved some of the goals you set for yourself. If you have realized them all, that's wonderful. That means it's time to set some new ones. Always keep moving; don't stay in your comfort zone, but go forward. Realize that reaching goals is a milestone, but know that life is not the destination. It's the journey.

18. Be patient and content as you strive. If we never had to wait for anything, we would become spoiled, and we would quit trying. Good things come to those who wait. Be filled with excitement for your future as you enjoy your present.

"For I have learned in whatever state I am, to be content; I know how to be abased, and I know how to abound. Everywhere and in all things I have learned both to be full and to be hungry, both to abound and to suffer need. I can do all things through Christ who strengthens me" (Phil. 4:11–13).

Just like Paul, we must pray without ceasing, but we must also keep working every day toward our ultimate goals.

19. Everyone's outcome will be different. Perhaps it is not your role in life to find a Prince Charming, or a career, or be in business. Those things worked for me, and by reading my story, I hope you will discover your own unique purpose, and your own support system. Or jumpstart your purpose and give it a little rocket fuel now to take off. Go for it!

20. There is a story in the Bible in which Jesus heals ten lepers, but only one came back to thank Him "and with a loud voice glorified God" (Luke 17:11–19). Once you are healed from abuse, poverty, illness, or whatever your situation was, don't forget to say "thank you" to God and everyone who had a hand in helping you. One way to show thanks is to help someone else who is in your former situation. Hospital visits to strangers, even, to encourage them. If your finances permit, give a girl in an abusive situation a few dollars to help with her escape or get counseling, or bring materials to her from a support group. Pray with her. Loan her this book. Remember what you needed when you were the victim, and give it to someone else. But be careful not to confront the abusive partner; do not put yourself in danger or become the victim of abuse again.

ONE BLACK EYE IS ONE TOO MANY

To women out there everywhere,
who live a life they will not share.
Hiding in a world of fear,
in their home they hold so dear.
Their self-esteem all stripped and bruised,
she never sleeps, she is abused.
By the one God said to love and honor,
now her marriage is full of horror.
How did it start, she wants to know;
she never thought she would let this go.
She loves her children so very much,
and would never want them to suffer such,

abuse from their chosen spouse,
when they grow up and leave her house.
The time is now to stop this pain,
actions speak and words are lame.
To her children who observe it all,
but are way to young to make the call,
To 911, please help us now,
the screaming, bleeding must stop somehow!
I'm a woman of value, I'm precious and dear,
God made me himself, I'll have nothing to fear.
From an evil heart who means me harm,
who bedazzled me with his dating charm.
Who now screams and yells and beats my face.
For him I pray God's saving grace,
but today's the day I leave this place.
Good-bye to him who brings me down,
makes me cry and makes me frown.
I celebrate God who made me whole,
made me special and healed my soul.
I am free of love so cruel and black,
I should have left him so far back.
Thank you Lord for letting me,
learn I'm worthy, you made me see.
That one black eye has no excuse,
no rhyme or reason, it is abuse!
You too deserve the very best,
take heed from me and all the rest.
Point your eyes to the Lord above,
all women deserve to have Real Love.
I pray for you, God's strength and power,
that you will not tarry one more hour.

Today's a new day, it's bright and clear,
so take your children ... *and get out of there!!!*

By Aurea McGarry
© 2007

PART III

Dealing With a Life-threatening Illness

Fifteen years before my surgery, if I had awaken to the news that I needed radically invasive surgery to attempt to remove a killer disease, I might have had cardiac arrest at that moment. The doctor was positive about removing 99 percent of the cancer, the ugly possibility remaining that the other 1 percent would have caused me to nag myself into ulcers, depression, and other illnesses. But I had spent years strengthening my personal faith, self-image, and self-respect. I had heightened my attitude and ambition and surrounded myself with people who loved and nurtured me. I had a desire to move forward regardless of the obstacles. What would you do if you were diagnosed with a possibly terminal disease? Here are a few suggestions and ideas that I learned from my experience with cancer.

1. Ask the doctors and medical staff questions. Find out all you can about the disease and about all your options—asking questions is the key. Ask for second, third, and fourth opinions; keep getting them until you are satisfied that you have left no stone unturned. There are specialists all over the world in almost every area of the medical field, and thanks to the Internet, we all have easy access to the information they can provide. So do not limit yourself to your hometown for answers, or for cures. Pray to God daily for wisdom and guidance, and he will direct your path. Remember, doctors are people, and not God.

Do not let doctors or anyone else in the medical field intimidate you. When I was diagnosed with cancer, one popular hospital to go to for cancer treatment was in Tampa. I had known several people who had gone there for treatment, and they were soon cancer-free, so I eagerly went to this hospital to have more tests done. One of the tests was a very painful biopsy in my lower back.

This bone marrow test is known for the pain it inflicts, since the patient has to be awake without any anesthesia. I have a very high tolerance for pain, and I knew I was in the best place possible. The doctor came in holding my chart, and he didn't seem very friendly. He asked why I was there.

"Isn't that my chart?" I asked. "Don't you know I'm having this test because they think I have cancer?"

He seemed confused, and not very positive or comforting. He didn't say anything else; he just rushed out and returned a few minutes later, and told me to turn on my stomach and brace for pain. My husband asked if I could have something topical to reduce the pain, and he abruptly shot back a "no." Then he took out a long needle to suck the bone marrow out of my spine.

It was the most intense pain I have ever felt; I wanted to scream, and tears flowed down my face as I squeezed Brian's hands until they were numb. Poor Brian wanted to help me, but he couldn't. Then, both the doctor and nurse left and said someone would be in shortly to give me something for the pain. We waited for almost an hour as my pain begin to intensify. Brian went up and down the hall trying to find a nurse that would give him at least an aspirin or something for the pain. It took him fifteen minutes to find someone to help him. Finally, I was given some pain pills, and we left.

When we returned a few days later for the results of the test, no one knew who I was because they had lost my chart. The hospital staff on duty that day was different than those who were there during my earlier visit. I was frightened. I didn't have a sore throat or a sprained ankle—I possibly had cancer. I wondered if I would make it through the following six months being treated like that. At that point, I didn't care how good the hospital's reputation was; I didn't want to be treated like a number with a lost chart. I was a person with a name. Brian then took my hand and said, "Let's get out of here, now."

We were at a loss at what to do next, but as we were driving over the beautiful waters on the Howard Franklin bridge, my cell phone rang. It was my ex-husband calling to find out the results of the test. I told him about our horrible experience, and he said something that would again change my life. God can use the most unexpected people at the most unexpected times to touch our lives and help. Anthony's sister was married to an oncologist, and he said he would have him call me. Soon, the doctor called and told me about an oncologist who used to work at the hospital we had just left but had started his own practice. He said this doctor didn't feel it was comforting for a cancer patient to see a different doctor each time, and he wanted to build rapport with his patients. This sounded more like a doctor I wanted to see.

Plus, the hospital we were leaving was more than an hour from our house, but this doctor was only five minutes from home—more good news.

We went to see Dr. Knipe at Gulf Coast Oncology, and we were greeted by a friendly staff. The doctor saw me right away. I will never forget when Dr. Knipe came into the office and smiled. He said my cancer was curable and that I was going to be fine. He explained that chemotherapy would be difficult for me but that he would be there to help me through it. Then this busy oncologist spent more than an hour talking to us about how curable my cancer was and what I could expect. He answered all of our questions in detail and made us feel safe and assured. Dr. Knipe and his entire staff were special people in our lives, and will be forever. They made my days with cancer bearable by treating us like family.

So never let a doctor make you feel guilty for asking too many questions, or getting a second, third, or fourth opinion. It is your body and your health, and you need to be in control. God bless you, Dr. Knipe, for your work with cancer patients. And thank you for never losing my chart!

2. Being diagnosed can make you feel helpless. Take a deep breath and a short walk, or sit quietly in a church and clear your head. Also, get on every prayer chain you can. Brian was calling every pastor and evangelist he knew of who believed in faith healing and the power of prayer for total restoration. It is amazing that you can really feel the power of people's prayers. It is a warm peace and joy inside your spirit that is unexplainable and wonderful.

I felt the prayers so strongly that I began to feel a peace and energy. It was so uplifting to get calls from people who would pray with me over the phone. They would claim God's healing for me, and it gave me the strength to endure it all. If you don't have anyone to pray with you, get on a prayer line with your church, or any other church that believes in the power of prayer for physical healing. You can go to my Web site to find some of my favorites.

Fear is normal. You will no doubt work hard to be brave for those around you, which is good. But every now and then, you will see that black shadow coming toward you, and it will chill you to your spine. It is like a black cloud that covers the sun. And you will ask yourself, "Am I going to die? Will the treatment be more than I can stand? Will I be disfigured?"

We have been taught as a society to fear cancer. We read so much about cancer taking lives. Novels have been written in which the main character—the patient—dies. Hollywood is a great love of mine, but it hasn't helped the cancer patient. In so many of the movies, the person with cancer dies, or the movie portrays the characters celebrating their last Christmas together and saying their good-byes. But look at some new findings: Cancer Research UK stated online that figures show a patient with cancer now has a 46.2% chance of being alive ten years after diagnosis, compared with 23.6% thirty years ago. Early detection, special surgeries, and more advanced chemotherapy drugs have attributed to this. I had a terrible time with the chemo, but not everyone does. New drugs are provided for nausea, and there are other buffering drugs available, too.

President Franklin D. Roosevelt once said, "The only thing we have to fear is fear itself." Fear is naturally a big part of any illness, but you shouldn't let the fear take over. In some cases, it has even caused some men and women to not seek treatment.

So don't watch those movies; stick with comedies, and put the casualties out of your mind. In any war, there are casualties, but the survivors come home to a new life. Maybe they have lost a limb or some other part of their bodies, but they are grateful to be alive, and they take what they have and run with it. Illness is also a war, but be careful in the combat zone. Have a courageous heart, and you will be a survivor. Illness is one of the sad things in this world, but remember what is written in 1 John 4:4: "He who is in you is greater than he who is in the world."

3. Don't try to go it alone. Surround yourself with people who love you; find a good support group. When I was going through my mother's things, I found a diary in which she wrote: "I have been diagnosed with lung cancer and have only a few weeks to live." In the corner, she had written "Dr. K in Michigan … helps people die."

She was referring, of course, to Dr. Jack Kevorkian, the famed suicide doctor.

I cry every time I read that. She had Eric, and he was wonderful to her, but I wonder what was going through her mind at that time she wrote that. I think she may have feared long suffering. Don't isolate yourself. Find a close friend, or a new friend, or a pastor or group you can talk with. The American Cancer Society can help: 1-800-ACS-2345. Or check the Internet for www.cancer.org and www.cancersurvivors.org.

I am so blessed to have the same best friend—Lisa—since I was a teenager. Although a controlling husband and an abusive situation kept us apart for a few years, our bond was too strong to keep us apart forever. During those years apart, I thought of her so often. I missed our talks and lunches, and I always wondered what she was doing. No matter how controlling a person may be, they cannot control your heart or erase your memories.

During our years apart, Lisa married Ron Skinner, a handsome, brown-eyed man who rocked her world. He was a drummer in our favorite local rock band when I was in college in Florida. They now have three awesome children: Brittany, Bradley, and Brooke. They are like my own children, and I consider little Brooke, the youngest, to be my junior best friend.

Although Lisa and I now live a state apart, I pick up the cell phone and call her almost daily. We laugh and cry together all the time—it is a girl thing. We have many things in common, but we have our differences, too, and that helps us balance our lives. She has given me the courage not to let others take advantage of me. She taught me that I could be a sweet, loving person and still not be a doormat for others to walk on. She is strong where I am weak, and I am strong where she is weak. We are each other's best cheerleaders, and we embrace each other's differences, which makes us a stronger team. We love each other unconditionally, and knowing we have each other makes everything more bearable.

A load is much lighter when shared by two. In order to have a best friend, you must *be* a best friend—and the rewards are priceless.

Our annual family vacation in Tennessee. Left to right: Bradley, Brittany, Ron, Lisa, Brian, me, Angelica, and her fiancé, Morgan. In front, Brooke and Alyssa.

My dad, Eric, talks about my mother's cancer in an e-mail to me:

> Aurea, your mother first got lymphoma in 1983. The doctors said they could remove it, but she didn't want to have surgery. The first doctor told her that they could remove the tumor, but her jaw would droop and she would have no feeling on that side. We got a second opinion and she was introduced to the Macrobiotic diet. While she was on the diet, she got radiation treatment and oral steroids that reduced the cancer in size. After much research, she chose not to have that particular surgery, and made a full recovery. We believe the diet helped prevent the cancer from returning.
>
> About twelve years later, she was diagnosed with liver and lung cancer, and given two months to live. I convinced her to get another opinion, and the doctor then said "there is always a chance."
>
> My opinion is that everything should be in moderation, and there is always that chance. The will to live is a great prevention. I firmly believe that if we

can master our thoughts, we can accomplish anything we want—even destroying negative outside forces such as cancer.

When I heard Doric had cancer, I thought, "not so soon ... but with his smarts he will beat it." And when I heard you had cancer, I knew you were strong-willed and had great strength in your faith and you too would defeat it, but—wow. What you would have to go through! I am sorry I was not there with you, but with Brian, I knew you were in really good hands.

I would tell anyone with a terminal illness that it isn't over until the fat lady sings. A person always has a chance to survive. The will must be very strong, and it helps to have friends and relatives who are your side to give you support and positive words. I believe people with positive words and faith, like you and Brian, will be above things. I also believe that laughter is a great immune booster. We share this in common. We always can find some way to make each other laugh at some point.

Another thing I believe in is working out and nutrition. Start now. The body is like a car. You put premium gas into it, keep the engine tuned, and check the tires, and the car will go on forever. You may get a flat tire or a damaged fender, but the inside is what makes it go.

4. Laugh! Even with a depressing illness, try to keep your sense of humor. Laughter is the best medicine. I remember Brian was best at prescribing humor. One day, I was lying in my private hospital room after one of my treatments. I was there for five days with a potassium drip IV to prevent me from vomiting eighteen times a day for ten straight days. Brian was well experienced with the hospital stay and knew just what to bring me: things like chocolate pudding and VCR tapes. Brian was setting up the VCR to the hospital television. The hospital television got only a few channels, so he brought me movies to watch instead.

With my favorite movies on tape—Brian was adjusting the TV and placing the VCR on the shelf, when I heard him say "Ooops!" I saw the lip of the shelf had broken off the wall. I told him not to worry about it and that someone from maintenance would come to repair it.

Brian looked around the room and came up with a great idea. He came over to my hospital tray, where the food lay uneaten, as usual, and took a spoonful of the mashed potatoes. He put it on the wood, and stuck it back on the wall.

"Well, eating them wasn't an option, was it?" he said. "They might as well serve a *useful* purpose."

I was laughing so hard it hurt! I thought the shelf would fall off again in a few hours, but it didn't. Day after day, I watched as the mashed potato glue held the shelf to the wall. Leave it to Brian to think of something like that—and to have it work.

But the funniest part is that when I came back to the same room three weeks later for my next treatment. The mashed potatoes were still holding the shelf to the wall, and no one had noticed. So thanks to my husband the true purpose of hospital mashed potatoes has been discovered: it is a household plaster.

Use it in good health.

5. Don't wait. Get into treatment as soon as possible, and never let chronic pain go undiagnosed. Pain is a way the body alerts you that something is wrong. Whether it's cracked ribs, pulled muscles, or the flu, find out why you are in pain.

I don't want to hear a doctor say, "It is probably …" I want to know for sure. I will take pain medications when I know what is wrong, but I don't want to use them to cover up some mystery illness. There are so many cures now for illnesses if they are diagnosed early, so if your body is in pain, figure out the cause. It's better to be safe than sorry.

One important thing I did after being diagnosed with cancer was to begin vitamin therapy. "Better late then never," I thought. I did it to get ready for chemotherapy, but I put it on hold during the chemo so it wouldn't interfere with some of those drugs. But after chemo was over, I went back to massive vitamin regimens. I took minerals, organic juices, organic coffee enemas, and then chelatian therapy. Some doctors use chelation to treat hardening of the arteries. The safety and efficacy of EDTA chelation therapy as a treatment for coronary artery disease are being assessed by NCCAM in a five-year study which began in 2002. It is also used to help remove heavy metals from the body like lead, arsenic, and mercury. Although this is all controversial, and many would argue that it is not going to help, Brian and I decided that it couldn't hurt to do something to clean out my body after all those cancer-fighting drugs were put in. We still take many vitamins, protein shakes, and supplements to this day. Like my oncologist said, "A balanced vitamin regime won't hurt you, and if it makes you feel good, then great."

6. Don't slip into denial. God is not the author of illness and disease. He came to deliver us. We become like pure gold after going through the fires and tribulations of life, and although God allows us to go through these hard times, it will make us stronger if we allow it to make us better in some way.

We hate hearing it when we are going through tough times, but everything *does* happen for a reason. We may never know the reason, and bad things happen to good people every day. It would be easy to be angry with God, but just remember, He is not the author of it, but He will lead you through it. Seek Him with all your heart and He will help you. He will also help you to help others who are going through a similar experience. If we try to help each other with what our experiences have taught us, and reach out with helping hands and helping hearts, the world could be so much better.

Your attitude will determine your altitude in life, so choose to have a good one no matter what. And if you don't have one now, strive to get one. You can do it!

7. I have learned from my business colleagues that attitude is half the battle; positive thinking can make a difference. You are going to get well, no matter what the diagnosis. Why not believe in a miracle? Why not a miracle for you? Whether we receive one or not, we live each day better for keeping hope alive. It certainly won't hurt.

I know you may have gained or lost a lot of weight. Even if you aren't getting dressed these days, put on a cute pair of pajamas, a nice bed-jacket, or even a T-shirt that says, "I'm sexy." Bring your chair near the window so you can see the sun, or, if it is a nice day, sit on the patio or porch. Brush your hair, or if you have lost your hair, find a nice turban or a glamorous wig. And remember that hair and eyelashes grow back.

Wear your cologne, put on a little makeup, and make an effort to see friends when you feel like it. You need your support group. If someone starts telling you a negative story about someone who died with what you have, stop them and tell them you don't want to hear that. People also die while crossing the street, so what difference does it make? You only want to hear positive things. Positivity builds up; negativity tears down.

Pets are also great support pals and are always positive friends, as long as someone else can meet their needs with food, water, exercise, and such. A kitty or puppy sitting on your lap can be a great confidant, so tell the pet your fears and your secrets. I promise, they won't tell a soul. What a great source of unconditional love.

Remain busy, keeping your mind on other things. Watch your favorite television programs, especially ones that make you laugh, or check out some old movies. Read a novel or some inspirational material. Work a puzzle. If you are up to it, make scrapbooks. This is a great way to catalog all those family photographs, and in doing so, it will bring back some happy memories. And try to keep a journal. One day, you will look back and think, "Was that *my* life? Did I really make it through that?"

8. I have experienced that prayer changes things, so ask for the prayers from others, and pray yourself. God will hear you. He heard me crying in the wilderness. Learn to lean on the Lord, knowing that everything in life changes, and miracles do happen. We must learn to be able to change, too. The bud changes into the flower, the seed into the fruit, and the caterpillar into the butterfly. The only thing in life that does not change is God: "He is the same yesterday, today and forever" (Heb. 13:8). And then stand on your faith knowing that what you are going through is only for a season. "To everything there is a season, a time for every purpose under heaven" (Eccles. 3:1).

9. Develop your inner beauty. I am in a cosmetics field, and I know how important it is for women to look their best in order to feel their best, but there is an inner beauty.

Have you ever heard that when a woman is pregnant, she glows? I think that is true, because she's carrying something wonderful and beautiful inside her: a new life. But we carry something else inside all of us: God's love. Our bodies are temples of God, so we, too, have a reason to glow.

I know someone who has a friend who had cancer on her nose four times. Her job called for her to constantly be in the public eye, so she had always took great pride in her appearance. After the cancer surgeries, she had to wear a bandage on her face for a long time. She laughed and called herself "the mask," and told everyone she would be fine once the bandages came off. But she wasn't. A huge scar covered her nose.

She went to a plastic surgeon, hoping this was an option to fix it. The doctor said he could do surgery, but that there was a 30 percent chance it would not help, a 30 percent chance it would look great, and 30 percent chance it would look worse, and a 10 percent chance the cancer would return. So she went for a second opinion, and the second surgeon said he would not do the surgery at all, for fear of having to remove too much of the nose and interfering with her breathing.

So she decided against the surgery and went home to have a pity party. What was she going to do? Was she going to quit work? She had to stand up in front of people and give talks and presentations all the time. She was very much in the public eye, and her photo often appeared in the newspaper. She really couldn't afford to quit work, so she went to God in Prayer.

She said, "God, I know you don't look at the outside, only the inside. But everyone else looks at the outside. I can't even look in the mirror with out feeling self-pity. How am I going to get up in front of a crowd and give a presentation?"

Slowly, the answer began to come to her, without her realizing it. She purchased some new eyeglasses and a new suit, got a new haircut, and changed her nail polish from the usual red to pink. Sure, she was scared that first day, but she knew God was with her. She breezed into the conference room and told everyone how she had missed them, and how special and talented they were. She told them all that they were wonderful, and to get out there and go to work.

Well, after the presentation, everyone came to compliment her on her glasses, her hair, and her clothes, and all of them kept looking at her, saying that there was something different. They couldn't figure out what it was, but they all told her that they had missed her so much, and that she had always made them feel so special.

She soon realized that eventually, people won't remember what you looked like, what you wore, or even what you said. But they never forget how you made them feel. If you made them feel good about themselves, they remember, and they know you care about them. I learned a very important and true statement in my career training classes: "They don't care how much you know, until they know how much you care."

From that day on, no one even mentioned her nose. All the love and caring was still there, just as it had been before the surgeries. And she excelled at her job more than ever. The scar is still there, of course, but she thinks about Jesus's nail-scarred hands and spear-scarred side. His scars were the ways his disciples recognized him in the resurrection, and they were placed there because of his love for us. Today when she looks in the mirror, she doesn't even notice her scar.

10. It is also important to make use of whatever time we have. If one dies at twenty, or eighty, the chronological years are not as important as what we accomplished *during* those years. On your tombstone or marker will be written: "*Born in 19---Died in 20--*. But that one little dash, between your birth date and the date of your death, is what really counts. What you do during that dash—the years you were alive—is what counts, no matter how long or short that time span may be.

We see what a role model Christopher Reeves was from his wheelchair; he was more of a real Superman than he ever was on the movie screen. Some people's epitaph should read, "Died at twenty-five and buried at seventy-five," because during the years in between they did nothing but drift—they were dead and didn't even know it.

So have a little attitude adjustment, fight, and make a difference while you are here on Earth.

My brother Doric and I both survived cancer. Doric had this to say when I asked him for words of advice on this subject:

> Aurea and I had very different types on cancer, but it was weird that we had it almost at the same time. I don't know if it was genetic or environmental. I really don't know why we got it. Maybe it is all just part of the "ride" of life, and I needed the benefits of the ordeal. Who knows? I don't blame myself, though; it was way out of my control.
>
> All emotions have cycles: anger cycles, depression cycles, hate cycles, joy cycles. There are also relationship cycles, project cycles, and many more. They all have different qualities and duration, and they vary between individuals. For instance, some grieve and recover in a short period of intense emotion, while others take longer, with their emotion less dramatic. Working to help people open up to their natural cycles can free up a lot of energy that can be used for healing and other useful activities. Very often, people waste energy by trying to hold back their cycles for various reasons, usually involving fear and shame.

Doric is listed in *Psychology Today*. He is a marriage and family therapist. Go to my Web site to read more of what he has to say.

11. Set goals for yourself. Think positive. Only three more chemo treatments … only one more surgery … only one more transplant … only one more transfusion … whatever. See the cup as half full, never as half empty.

"For a great and effective door has opened to me and there are many adversaries" (I Cor. 16:9).

We all have adversaries, but Galatians 3:4 says, "Have you suffered so many things in vain?" Well, don't let it be for nothing. Grow in spirit and truth. Whatever your situation is now, it is only temporary. Life is always changing, and you can keep it moving forward toward your goals and dreams. The truest thing about life is, we are just passing through. So live your legacy now!!

12. Live in the moment. You are alive today, so what can you do today to make some memories? Who can you be an inspiration to? What can you do today that you always wanted to do, or meant to do, that you have not yet done?

Setting goals is necessary to continue living, but we also must live in the present. Too often, we live in the past or the future, but we also must learn to live now. Remember, as it is written in Matthews 6:34: "Do not worry or be anxious about tomorrow, for tomorrow will have worries and anxieties of its own, sufficient for each day is its own trouble."

Don't waste your "now" by worrying about tomorrow. You can work for the future, but live for today. Elizabeth Edwards, the wife of presidential candidate John Edwards, was diagnosed with breast cancer years ago, and it returned. When John Edwards told his children about the cancer, he said, "If anyone here is not going to die … raise your hand." No one raised his or her hand.

Some people diagnosed with cancer *will* die from it, but many will not, and more are surviving and thriving every year. Elizabeth Edwards went ahead with her husband's campaign. It is good to stay focused on something positive, and I am sure it keeps her mind off her illness, as she lives for today with a purpose and inspires the rest of us to do the same.

13. Tell your family how much you love them and how much you appreciate their support. A famous doll artist died in 2006, and on her tombstone they inscribed: "She enjoyed life." That is important, too.

Yes, we have important work to do, but in doing so, God intended for us to enjoy life. Even though heaven may be our desired destination, God wants us to enjoy the journey of our lives here on Earth.

"It is good and fitting for one to eat and drink and to enjoy the good of all his labor in which he toils under the sun all the days of his life which God gives him, for it is his heritage" (Eccles. 5:18).

14. Focus on taking care of yourself and getting well, but focus on others, too. Sometimes when we get out of ourselves and work on enriching the lives of others, it helps. We must realize that the battles we face in life are not only our battles but God's as well. If we stop relying only on ourselves and also rely on God, God will help us win the battle.

In 2 Kings 4, we can read about a woman who had to empty herself to be used by God, and she filled many other empty people. I am grateful to have been able to have my own business, and I could give myself a raise anytime by working harder. This gave me the opportunity to help my brother when he needed it the most. Doric was a full-time massage therapist when he was diagnosed with Hodgkin's. The massage field is very physically demanding, so he couldn't work as much during his chemotherapy and radiation treatments. How glad I was to be successful enough in my career to have enough extra money to give some to him for his support while he was focusing on getting well.

A very successful woman in our business once said that having money is not a bad thing, because it buys you choices. So try to put aside a little extra money.

Someday, someone you love may need a little extra help, and you can provide it. Sometimes, God calls on us to make a difference.

15. What can you do to make a difference? When we do the work the Lord has planned for us to do, he will give us the energy. If you want to do the will of God, you must get involved with other people. We need to make sure our plan lines up with God's. Learn and listen to know God's plan for you. "For I know the thought and plans I have for you, says the Lord, thoughts of peace and not for evil, to give you a future and a hope" (Jeremiah 29:11).

16. Remember, you have been saved and called for a purpose—so find it. Today is the first day of the rest of your life. "This is the day that the Lord has made; we will rejoice and be glad in it" (Ps. 118:24)

PART IV
My Life Today

Today, my life is extremely busy, but I am so glad to be living it. Sometimes I don't believe there are enough hours in the day; I am a wife, mother, grandmother, speaker, author, and a successful businesswoman with a large team of women working with me.

As of 2007, I have earned the use of seven company cars. I attend church and study the Bible to grow spiritually every day. I judge beauty pageants whenever possible. I am a sought-after motivational speaker. We love to travel, and I am now writing books to help others.

My body, which once felt like coal and all used up, now feels like silver. Do you know how silver is made? A silversmith holds the ore in the hottest part of the flames but never takes his eye off the ore, because if he leaves it a moment too long it is destroyed. He knows the silver is refined once he can see his reflection in it.

I, too, have been through the fire. But now, I hope people can see God's grace shining through me. I've come a long way, baby, as you can see. Yes, God healed me, inside and out. But I also had to make myself get out of bed and take those first steps every day. You can too—I believe in you.

Virginia Woolf once said, "To let oneself be carried on passively is unthinkable."

Epilogue

In another few years, when I have reached the top position in my career, I will write another book. I think we all have a book inside us and a story to tell. And as I finish this first book, I am receiving the news that my daughter might be having her turn with cancer. She will be going through some diagnostic tests in August 2007 to determine her condition. Her positive attitude has been amazing. She has lived most of my life with me and lives and breathes faith, overcoming any obstacle. She will be strong, and she will make it through with flying colors, because that is what she has learned from our faith-filled lives.

I love what Mark Twain once said: "When I die, I want to be totally used up." I, too, want to accomplish everything I set out to accomplish, and I have shared so much along the way. By then, my beautiful granddaughter will be older, and there will be so much I will want to share with her. I hope abuse and cancer will not be a part of her life, but if they are, I want her to know that whatever comes her way, she can—and will—thrive.

Isaiah 43:2 says, "When you pass through the waters I will be with you, and through the rivers, they will not overflow you. When you walk through the fire, you will not be burned nor shall the flame scorch you."

Remember Daniel in the lion's den; God promises the same kind of help to all of those who trust in him. One of the greatest feelings is living the life you want to live, complete with the good times and the bad, but nevertheless shaped by your own choices and not someone else's.

I am so proud of my family, and I hope they are proud of me, too. But more importantly, when I come to the end of my journey, I want to hear Jesus say to me, as he said in Matthew 25:21, "Well-done, my good and faithful servant … enter into thy just reward,"

978-0-595-45369-6
0-595-45369-4